Paul Barrington

Gems of knowledge

Paul Barrington

Gems of knowledge

ISBN/EAN: 9783337257903

Printed in Europe, USA, Canada, Australia, Japan

Cover: Foto ©Andreas Hilbeck / pixelio.de

More available books at **www.hansebooks.com**

GEMS OF KNOWLEDGE.

COMMON SENSE PRESCRIPTIONS AND PRACTICAL INFORMATION.

A SYSTEMATIC TREATMENT IN THE DOMESTIC PRACTICE OF
MEDICINE.

By PAUL J. BARRINGTON, M. D. & CO,

SOLD BY THE AUTHOR AND HIS AGENTS ONLY.

CHICAGO:
OTTAWAY & COMPANY, PRINTERS,
54 & 56 FRANKLIN STREET.
1881.

THIS BOOK IS DEDICATED

To our much-loved and esteemed Friend and Brother,

Z. W. BINGHAM, M. D.

PREFACE.

The object of placing this volume (as its title indicates) before the public and non-professional class of people, is to furnish them with a few useful hints and suggestions for those who are sick as well as those who care for the sick.

In the practice of over twenty years by the bedside of the sick and unfortunate, we have long since felt impressed with the necessity of a more practical work that may be placed in the hands of *all*— a book of useful *knowledge*, stripped of all technicalities, clothed with the plainest common-sense language, which contains the most practical and useful information upon all subjects pertaining to the physical well-being of all—from infancy to old age—as the general knowledge they impart, the instructions they give for the preservation of health, comfort and happiness, are worth more than all the strong medicines in the world. This book is not intended to take the place of a physician, when one is really needed. Oh, no! but more especially to instruct you to know and do many things that are highly necessary for you as well as the physician, together with other useful informa-

(3)

tion, such as we feel will be highly prized in every home. In order to satisfy the demands of all progressive minds of the present day, in regard to their choice in the many schools of medical practice, we have combined the homœopathic system of medication, which has within the last few years become so successful and popular, together with some of the most important remedies that are known in medical science up to the present day.

By the Author.

INTRODUCTION.

In giving the homœopathic treatment, it is our desire to be concise, and not give remedies enough to confuse the mind in choosing from the many, which we think has been a great error in the profession. Our object is to shorten the list, and choose the best remedies for the various diseases of which we will speak, making it more practical and admissible to every household. Careful study for years has been the means of developing these thoughts, together with the practical experience in life, drawn from the bedside of the sick and afflicted; from the palace to the hovel in consultation with some of the leading physicians of the present day; in fact; from all phases of life. Therefore, it is our wish to be as brief and simple as possible in aiding humanity; trying to encourage and assist them to acquire and maintain a thorough knowledge of their entire physical body, and the laws that govern—fully understanding if these sacred laws are violated the physical *must* suffer. With this knowledge put into practice the whole system may be kept in a healthy condition and all the complex machinery brought into active play, and the results

can only produce a appy influence with those
they come in contact, while a deseased body cannot contain a happy, contented spirit—hence, the
great need of more light in this direction.

The remedies in this department will be chosen
from the active principle of each drug. Our remedies are procured only from the leading homœopathic pharmacies of large cities: H. C. Luytus,
No. 306 North Fifth Stréet, St. Louis, Mo.; Boer-
ick & Tafel, No. 35 Clark Street, Chicago, Ill.; also
Gross & Delbridge, No. 48 Madison Street, Chicago, Ill. These are good reliable firms. If there
should be a homœopathic physician in your vicin-
ity all necessary remedies can be obtained from
him. In ordering medicine you should be careful
and state distinctly what you wish; whether it be
Mother Tincture or the decimal dilutions. Perhaps an explanation in regard to the attenuations
may be necessary in order for you to understand
our method of administering medicines. The
name and strength are usually labeled on the vial.
Below we will give a short description of the
marked characters that will enable you to choose
what strength may be called for, in certain cases:
When you see a character marked *thus* ⏀ it denotes
full strength, or Mother Tincture, regardless of
name, and from this all other decimal attenuations
are made.

Thus:

3.x in any drug means the third attenuation.

6.x. "   "   "   " sixth   "

12.x. "   "   "   " twelfth   "

30.x. " ·   "   "   " thirtieth   "

and so on, up to the five-thousandth (a point we have not yet been able to attain) or advocate; time and experience may reveal the beautiful spiritual action of practical truth. In ordering medicine you should give name and state the strength desired. For an illustration: Tincture Aconite ∅ one ounce; Aconite 3.x, half ounce, and so on the dose will be given under each disease, and can be referred to in the book. We prescribe the dilution from the fact of their being better understood than the triturations (or powders). When prepared in water it should be renewed every day. Neither would we advise the medicated globules for home practice, as has been done in the past, for we feel they are not so effectual unless medicated by ourselves at the time of prescribing. Many of our remedies through the book will be abbreviated to save time and space. Thus:

Acon.   for Aconite.

Bell.   " Belladonna.

Gels.   " Gelseminum.

Bry.   " Bryonia.

Cal. Carb. " Calcaria Carbonica.

Puls.   " Pulsatilla, etc., etc.

In presenting this book to the public, it is with a hope that it will be accepted as a guide to the multitude of people throughout the land, and especially those in the plainer walks of life, who have limited opportunities of becoming acquainted with the latest and best method of treating themselves. If we can accomplish this we shall feel our efforts have not been in vain; what the result will be, time and the readers of our book must decide. The motive was for the best good of all. V. V. BARRINGTON, M. D.,

Homœopathic Department.

HOW TO NURSE THE SICK.

We commence this book with the above to state plainly their qualifications and duties, for we know the success of the remedies applied to the sick depend almost wholly upon the *nurse*, and it is generally conceded or admitted that a good nurse and a poor physician are more successful than a poor nurse and a good physician. The art of nursing is a natural gift and cannot be wholly acquired, yet it may be much improved or developed by close observation and study. There are many reasons why we have so few good nurses. 1. *A nurse* may be too young, and also too old. The first is apt to be thoughtless, wild and heedless; the latter may be deaf, stupid, or in trouble. Good nurses should always be able to control themselves under all circumstances. But no matter who the nurse may be, she should always enter the sick room with a cheerful face and a sweet smile, no matter how grave the case. She should be gentle, kind and tender; always calm, not excitable; must have a pleasant voice, a gentle, magnetic touch, a light, easy step, and a knowledge of preparing food for the *invalid*. Such a nurse is invaluable.

2. She should be honest both with the patient and the physician.

(9)

3. If the patient have no confidence in the nurse, the sick room is no place for such an individual; or if the conduct be such as to lead the physician to think his orders have not been attended to, it surely is a very unpleasant place to occupy. But no person should employ a physician unless they have full confidence in his ability, after which they should understand his directions and be sure his orders are carefully and faithfully executed. Some nurses fancy they know far better what is necessary than the physician, and in order to carry out their plans they resort to a species of dishonesty. Such nurses should be entirely avoided, for they ought to know and understand that the patient must suffer and, perhaps, die from such treatment.

4. *A nurse should be dignified and genteel.* Some are always in a constant giggle; the grin of childish levity and thoughtless noise, and roaring laughter should be avoided; in fact, no person should be allowed in a sick room who cannot manifest perfect self-control. The next quality should be *firmness;* every nurse should be resolute, but not rude. It is not expected that she should yield to every request of the patient unless it coincide with reason and common sense; but what she does should be done cheerfully and kindly, as well as carefully; then the patient will have confidence in her ability for exercising her good judgment.

5. The next thing of importance is patience. It requires a very large degree, for the reason that invalids are often irritable and restless, and sometimes well persons may partake of their influence. Please remember this. Have you not frequently chided yourself for your own impatience under certain circumstances? *We have.* Then how could you expect it otherwise with those who are suffering and compelled to stay in bed for weeks, perhaps months, and be deprived of their liberty and enjoyment, even walking about the house? Therefore it does not matter how sorely tried and worn out the nurse may be, it does not furnish an excuse for getting out of patience. A nurse should *always possess gentleness*, especially in case of a broken limb, painful back, or rheumatism, etc. When it is necessary to change the clothes great tenderness and gentleness should manifest itself. The invalid should always be handled with a steady hand; the hold that insures firmness, strength and gentleness will insure confidence in the patient and make him feel secure. This duty should always be performed with a spirit of kindness and sympathy, and not in a rough, uncouth manner.

6. *The most important of all is cleanliness.* The nurse should not only be clean herself, but she should keep the room clean and sweet. The room should be well ventilated with fresh air and sunlight, and not from inner rooms or halls; the best

way is to let the window down from the top; the
air should not come directly upon the patient, but
the room should always be kept with an even temperature (or heat). Vessels containing particles of
food should never be allowed to remain in the
room. Drinking water should be changed as often
as called for, as it gathers impurities by standing.
With careful attention to the little things connected with the sick room, any nurse will be amply
rewarded by the speedy recovery of her patient.

7. Some people are too generous and indulgent
to make good nurses; they are always overwhelmed
in difficulties; they mean to be good, but fail by
overdoing. She many times comes loaded down
with good things, both hands full; in trying to get
up-stairs she steps on the bottom of her dress, drops
a plate, spills the tea, or, perhaps, falls herself.
With a great effort she manages to get up, and
places what she has left on the tray before the
patient. In her hurry and confusion she cuts the
bread and butters it with a knife that has previously
been used to cut an onion or spread a mustard plaster, and says: "Now, dear, I will go back and
make some more tea." The patient asks for a
drink of water before she goes. She says, "Yes,
dear," and runs off, gets a glass brim full, puts her
hand under the patient's head, bends his neck, and
turns the water down on the outside, all over the
breast and clothing. Then she wonders why in the

world he don't drink better. In lighting the lamp
she uses a bit of paper, then throws it on the floor
and stamps it out with her foot. The fire wants
fixing; she turns on too much fuel and it spills
over the floor; in trying to gather up the fragments
she leaves the stove door open till the room is filled
with smoke; in her hurry to relieve this condition,
the braid on her dress being loose it catches on the
chairs, and she drags them after her, making a
fearful noise, which is very annoying to the patient.
Her fingers are bound up with a rag tied with a
black string, having been scalded by trying to
pour hot water into the teapot. She forgets to give
the medicine at the right time. The soiled dishes
are left scattered all around the room, the food left
standing for hours by the bedside; the bed is full
of crumbs and seldom made up; the fire burns low
or goes out, the ashes strewn all over the hearth.
These things tend to annoy the patient, who becomes nervous; fever returns, and he gets no sleep
or rest during the night. Such a nurse means
well, but fails to accomplish the desired end from
lack of natural ability.

Every nurse should have good judgment and full
exercise of his or her senses.

Sight—To read directions, and sometimes to
read and amuse the patient.

Hearing—To catch the faintest whisper, to avoid
a great effort in speaking.

Feeling—To determine the change in temperature in the room, the heat of the body, the moisture or dryness of the skin, and to know when applications are to be made—when they are too cold
or too hot—to see that all drafts are avoided when
sponging or bathing the patient.

Smelling—To detect all effluvias or impurities
in the room.

Taste—To determine the seasoning of food.

A careful exercise of all natural faculties, with a
study of the principles of nursing, ought to make
a competent person to care for the sick.

ROOM FOR THE SICK.

It is not every family that has a choice of
rooms, but under all circumstances we must do the
best we can. A room should be selected that is
light and cheerful. The *head* of the bed should be
placed to the *north*, if possible, as the currents of
electricity in nature run from north to south. If
the patient has fever, brain disorder, or nervous
disease, let the room be in some quiet part of the
house, away from the family. If it be a bone
broken or fracture from the result of accident,
then the patient should be near the rest of the
family, for in such cases it is very often amuse-
ment for the patient to watch the movements

of the rest. Avoid a room that is exposed to any kind of effluvia, and have the windows so they can be let down at the top. The less furniture in the room the better, especially if the disease be infectious. Before putting the patient in the room see that it has been well aired, warmed and dried. First, light the fire and see that the chimney draws well. The best bed is a hair mattress, but clean straw or husks will answer very well. *Remember* that feather beds are not healthy; besides they are inconvenient, especially if the patient has a broken bone or fractured leg, and in wounds and burns—the patient is apt to sink down into holes. When the patient is to be changed and cannot get up, place him on the edge of the bed and roll up against him all the bed-clothes you intend to change, having your clean sheets and blankets all ready; spread them on the bed smooth and straight; get your patient to roll over carefully on the clean sheets; take off the soiled clothes, then spread out the other half of the clean ones. Now, don't you see, you have it all done nicely. If it be necessary to scour the room to purify it, wash it with hot water, first adding a few cents' worth of chloride of lime, or some carbolic acid. Then dry the room thoroughly and it is ready.

FOOD AND DRINK FOR THE SICK.

It will be necessary to know how to prepare certain kinds of food which the doctor may order for the patient. It is well for you to understand a few general principles that should govern the administration of food. First. Solid food is seldom admissible, especially during acute diseases of any kind, for the reason the stomach and digestive organs are not in a condition to furnish the fluids necessary for its comminution; hence, instead of digesting, it simply lies there and decomposes, which will give rise to irritation, and produce other serious complications. Second. The more severe the disease the more delicate and light the food should be. Thus, in high grades of fever or inflammation we should give whey, beef tea, extract of beef, milk punch, toast water, mutton broth, tapioca, chicken broth. Third. When there is great exhaustion the food should be all the more concentrated, and very nutritious. Then give the *Extract of Beef*, or beef essence, as it is sometimes called, chicken or mutton broth, milk and cream. Fourth. In fevers or inflammatory disease, give food at that period of the day or night when there is least vascular and nervous excitement, and never force it upon the patient if suffering from a high grade of fever. Fifth. Never give food during severe pain. Sixth. If the tongue be coated yellow, with bad taste in the mouth, a feeling of weight and oppression in the stomach, it is better not to give food; or if given, should always be in a liquid form. Seventh. When the digestion is impaired and it becomes necessary to sustain life with food, it should be given in small quantities and at regular intervals, like medicine, every two or three hours. Eighth. In convalescing much care is required in keeping the patient from eating too much.

RECIPES FOR COOKING.

BEEF TEA.

Take one pound of nice, tender steak, remove the fat, chop very fine, put it in a pint of cold water, stir, and let it soak one hour, then boil ten minutes, strain it and season to suit the taste of the patient.

EXTRACT OF BEEF.

Take a Scoth ale *stone* bottle (is the best), scald it out so that you know it is clean; take one pound of nice, tender, fat beefsteak; after removing the fat, chop it up fine, season it with a little salt and pepper, put it in the bottle, cork it up tight, then tie the cork down so that you know it will not fly out with the heat and steam: place the bottle in a *pot* of water and boil it for three

2

hours. Remember you cannot cook it too much. This preparation is very rich with nutritious element; two tablespoonfuls at a dose for an adult is sufficient, repeated every two or three hours. A little can be poured out at a time and warmed on the stove as it be required. Keep the bottle well corked; if it is left open the extract will lose much of its strength, as well as its flavor.

CHICKEN JELLY.

Take half a raw chicken, pound it well with a mallet, bones and all, cover it over with cold water; heat it slowly in a covered vessel; let it simmer till the meat is thoroughly cooked, then strain the liquor through a coarse cloth; season it to taste, return it to the stove and let it simmer ten minutes longer, skim it when cool and give it to the patient.

BARLEY WATER.

Take of pearl barley two ounces, boiling water two quarts, boil down to one quart and strain; a little lemon and sugar may be added. This is a good drink in all inflammatory and eruptive diseases, scarlet fever, measles, small-pox, etc.

RICE WATER.

Take of good rice two ounces, water two quarts, boil one and a half hours, then add sugar and nutmeg to suit the taste; use with milk. This is an excellent diet for children.

ARROWROOT JELLY.

One cup of boiling water, two teaspoonfuls of Bermuda arrowroot; wet the arrowroot in a little cold water and rub smooth, then stir it into hot water, which should be on the fire and boiling, with sugar already in it; stir until clear, then add one teaspoonful of lemon juice; wet a cup with cold water and pour the jelly, and let it form. Eat with sugar and cream, if you like.

BARLEY JELLY.

Boil one quart of water, let it cool; take one-third of a loaf of bread (common size), slice it up, pare off the crust. Toast it to a light brown, put it in the water in a covered vessel and boil it gently till you find, on putting some in a spoon to cool, that it becomes a jelly; now strain it and cool; add sugar and lemon juice, or grate a little lemon peel as it is used.

OATMEAL GRUEL.

Two tablespoonfuls of oatmeal, one quart water, boil ten minutes and strain; salt and sugar to suit your taste.

CORNMEAL GRUEL.

Made the same way, using cornmeal instead of oatmeal.

OATMEAL WATER.

Take two ounces of oatmeal, one quart of water, stir up well, let stand until settled, then drink the water with ice in it, if you choose. This is an excellent remedy for diarrhœa or in dysentery.

AGAIN.—Take milk one pint, sheep's suet three ounces, corn starch half an ounce, cardamon seeds one ounce, browned like you would coffee, then grind it very fine; after the other mixture is boiled gently for thirty minutes stir in the ground seed while it is yet hot; when cool it can be used as food and medicine. It is excellent. It will cure the very worst cases of dysentery or bloody flux. It does the work when the best of doctors fail.

BUTTERMILK PAP.

Take of fresh buttermilk four parts, water one part, mix and boil, then thicken with corn or oatmeal. Eat with butter and molasses.

WINE WHEY.

Heat a pint of new milk until it boils, at which moment pour in as much good wine as will curdle and clarify it; boil again and set aside until the curd subsides; pour off the whey carefully and add two pints of boiling water, and loaf sugar to suit the taste.

ORANGE WHEY.

Milk one pint, the juice of one orange with a

portion of the rind; boil the milk, then add the
orange juice; let stand till it coagulates, then
strain. Both of the above are excellent for conva-
lescent patients where there is weak digestion, for
children or adults.

VEGETABLE SOUP.

Take one potato, one turnip, and one onion, with
a little celery or celery seed; slice each, and boil
one hour in a quart of water; season to taste; then
pour the whole upon a piece of toast.

ELM-BARK JELLY.

Take two teaspoonfuls of finely pulverized elm-
bark and one pint of cold water; stir until a jelly
is formed; sweeten with loaf sugar. This is excellent for all diseases of the throat and lungs, coughs,
colds, etc. It is very nutritious.

FLAX-SEED LEMONADE OR COUGH SYRUP.

Four tablespoonfuls of whole flax-seed, half an
ounce horehound herb, one quart boiling water;
let steep for three hours in a covered vessel, and
strain the juice from three roasted onions and two
lemons; tincture of lobelia and ipecacuanha, of
each three drachms; add sugar to sweeten; if too
thick, add a little water. Partake of it freely; it
is excellent for colds, coughs, throat or lung. as
well as kidney trouble.

MILK PUNCH.

Take two fresh eggs, two tablespoonfuls loaf
sugar; beat well together on a plate; add one pint
of new milk, nutmeg and good brandy or whisky
to flavor it well. This is *par excellence* in low
grades of fever for children or adults. Change occasionally with the Extract of Beef, and the (see page
17) patient will live on them for days and weeks.

EATING.

The brain is interested in the process of digestion. If it be excited or over-taxed, or even vexed,
it will not stimulate the stomach to work till it is
rested. Never eat when you are mad, fatigued, or
exhausted. Drink a little gruel if you are very
hungry, then wait till you are rested before you
take a full meal. Always give the stomach time
to rest between meals. Always eat regularly. Frequent eating, as well as too frequent nursing of
children, soon weakens the stomach and liver, and
brings on dyspepsia and other kinds of disease.

Eat slowly.—Rapid eating, and drinking while
eating, is the curse of this nation. It produces
palpitation of the heart, vertigo, headache, neuralgia, nervous debility, spinal irritation, rheumatism,
premature old age. Chew your food thoroughly,
drink but little while eating, take plenty of time

—thirty minutes at each meal. Remember that stomach bitters will not chew your food for you. You are better off without such stuff.

Common lamentation.—" What is the cry of our fast-going people ? 'My food does not digest;' this is the saying all over America. 'My poor head aches half the time;' so exclaim our young ladies. ' My lungs are the best part of me, but my liver is diseased and torpid.' This is a popular complaint. 'And my bowels slow and sluggish.' Such miserable lamentations ascend from all the most fertile portions of this glorious continent. But we feel glad there is an awakening in the direction of physiological knowledge and universal improvement, and the final triumph will surely be: The triumphant conquest of individual man over all enemies to his bodily ease and mental tranquility.

" Is it not worthy of particular notice that the majority of people who, as invalids, incessantly complain in the department of digestion, are the most constant violators of physiological law? If any person should flatter him or herself that he or she can go on violating the conditions of *Health*, and at the same time, by simply yielding to the self-restoring mercies of his spiritual constitution, recover all his original vigor and bloom, his disappointment will be complete. Mother Nature is as loving and as just as Father God; but they do not, because they cannot, guarantee impunity from the effects of violation. All the medical isms, myths and pathies from Hippocrates down to the last nostram cannot perform the pardoning act. There is no infallible remedy, so you might as well pass the word all around the world —there is no specific for any human transgression. Let every eye read it, let every ear hear it, and inscribe it in fadeless characters upon the Temple of Health."—*Davis*.

LUNG LIFE; OR, PHYSIOLOGICAL FACTS.

The shortest route to health is through the lungs. Deprive them of heaven's invisible air, shut off the supply of the vivifying principle, and the whole beautiful machinery will immediately stop. Oxygen is universally the vehicle of heaven's divine breath ; these celestial elements ride straight through the lungs into the blood, thence to the great battery of all energy and digestion. The brain immediately distributes to each part of the body the principles of sensation, life and motion. To obtain this point, begin gradually and practice deep breathing daily, and you will find that the air is impregnated with an electric energy which pervades, refreshes, quickens and energizes every part of your physical temple. *Remember*, your food cannot digest, neither can your blood circulate, without the electric fire of the air; neither can a particle of food strengthen you without it. Without the living energy of the air, which is obtained through the lungs, no diet can be made universally nutritious. Salivary juice, as it pours out from the little springs on either side of the cheeks from the parotid glands, could do nothing without the vivifying electricity of the air. The gastric fluids —although loaded with its inherent pepsin and the acids, lactic, hydrochloric, etc., etc.—could accomplish nothing without a constant supply of nerve-energy. The lungs must absorb the electricity of the measureless immensity; otherwise nothing strong can occur, but death and transformation will hasten into the temple. Hence, the great necessity of reformation and knowledge in regard to these great facts, an unfolding of liberal ideas from the by-gone days of superstition and dogmas; when the old fashioned orthodox churches were built and kept as tight as drums during service. The result of ignorance; and narrowness of their creeds, concerning God and man.

In this connection we are reminded of Florence Nightingale, the noble nurse who voluntarily went to the Crimean war to bind up the bleeding soldiers. She says: "An extraordinary fallacy is the dread of night air. What air can we breathe at night but night air. The choice is between pure night air from without and foul night air

from within. Most people prefer the latter.
What will they say if it is proved to be true that
fully one-half the diseases we suffer from are occasioned by people sleeping with their windows
shut. An open window most nights in the year
can never hurt anyone. In great cities night
air is the best and purest out of the twenty-four
hours. We could better understand shutting the
windows in towns during the day than during the
night, for the sake of the sick; from the absence
of smoke and dust, as well as the quietude, all tend
to make the night air the best for aiding the sick.
It is impossible to keep well, and have good digestion, without pure air, and plenty of it; it
is also impossible to think large, manly, beautiful
and virtuous thoughts, while respiring in an
atmosphere of stagnation and consequent corrup-
tion. People who sleep in close, ill-ventilated
rooms are forever dreaming monotonous dreams,
loaded with vicious pictures, and animated by
strangers or demons, produced from the confined
air. Idiots breathe superficially; they seldom
respire like an intelligent mind. Timid persons
inhale small quantities of air. The coward has a
narrow chest, and he only uses the upper portion
of his lungs. Why does the strongest horse always have the broadest and deepest chest? The
mind cannot improve, morally and intellectually,
unless the lungs be large and full, constantly and

plentifully supplied with air. Health cannot be maintained in a confined atmosphere; no exalted thoughts, no spiritual perceptions, can manifest themselves.

PROCESS OF DIGESTION.

The Gastric Methods. The reasons in favor of full and intelligent respiration are numerous and easily understood. Chyle is the last result of fundamental digestion. But, in itself, chyle has no power to promote growth, give strength, or repair the waste of the body. It is the successor to chyme, which is manufactured from the food in the first part of digestion. It is first manufactured by the stomach into a pulpy mass, impregnated or charged with electricity of the vital kind. But when it passes downward into the lower stomach, or duodenum, the pancreatic fluids and the bile at once combine with it, thereby adding a positive element by which the chyme is transformed into a milk-white liquid (the chyle) and, with the residum, flows steadily into and through the small intestines. What next? The numerous mesenteric glands, with the lacteal vessels, commence their work of forming incipient eggs from out the chylic fluids; the unchylified portions (the residum) meantime passes onward into the large and lower bowels, and is then rejected, together with the broken-down blood globules, in the shape of bile and relative excretions. This material is wholly excrementitious.

The thoracic duct, so-called, conducts the chyle from the lacteal passages and mesenteric glands, and pours it into the vein which discharges its contents into the positive side of the heart.

PURIFYING ORDEAL OF THE BLOOD.

How is this accomplished? By means of the pure air of space. Yes; when heaven's devout breath enters the air-chambers the chyle is at once converted into nutritious blood, baptized to the multifarious necessities of the arterial system, while at the same time the cold venous blood is unloaded of its dead burdens in the form of carbonic gas and useless water. Carbon is the principal element of decay and death, yet is very essential to life and a good conductor to electricity. Therefore, the heart very wisely and energetically throws both the chyle and venous blood upon the entire responsibility of the lungs; so that when the invisible air is drawn by deep breathing into the pulmonary structure the divine life also enters, whereby the chyle is changed as by magic into the constructive principle for the soul's good, whereby the newly-purified blood is re-baptized and confirmed into the ways of righteousness; it hastens upon its mission of benevolence to all parts of the physical temple. Now, my dear reader, we feel that we have put this question in a light that you may understand fully the process of digestion, as well as the importance of lung life in health; the necessity of ventilation in the sick room; that you may better and more fully understand us when we speak upon the different conditions, in this book, How to Live, and what to do under all circumstances in disease and misfortune. For you should remember that nearly all diseases can be traced to the stomach and lungs, as the first origin from improper air and bad digestion.

; HOME MEDICINE CHEST.

Every family has more or less medicine about the house; but usually, they are kept carelessly sitting around no place in particular. It is well to have a small box, with a lock on it, and always kept in some convenient place. It would be useless for every house to keep a drug store; but it is well enough to keep a few reliable medicines, such as you would be likely to use in a case of emergency. But let me entreat you, never keep or buy any patent medicines, the ingredients of which are not known to you. There has been more damage produced by them than good accomplished; and, for the most part, they have been put up by ignorant pretenders, whose sole object is to get your money. Keep your castor oil, sweet oil, a vial of laudanum, a little tincture of lobelia, syrup of ipecac, spirits of camphor, a bottle of glycerine, and a vial of syrup of rhubarb. Keep in your chest a roll of lint, a roll of linen, a piece of flannel, and some sticking plaster. Have your physician put up a bottle of medicine for burns and scalds, and have a place for it in your chest. These are some of the medicines every family should keep on hand; not too many, only those which you know how to use. And for obvious reasons they should always be kept by themselves where they could be had at a moment's notice—all well labeled that you may make no mistake.

MEDICINES FOR A HAPPY HOME.

Not only should we cultivate such tempers as serve to render the intercourse of home amiable and affectionate, but we should strive to adorn it with those charms which good sense, judgment and refinement so easily impart to it. We say easily, for there are persons who think a home cannot be made beautiful without a considerable outlay of expense in money. Such people are in great error. It costs but very little to have a neat flower garden, and to surround your dwelling with those simple beauties which delight the eye far more than expensive objects. Nature delights in beauty; she loves to brighten the landscape and make it agreeable to the eye. She hangs the ivy all around the ruin, as well as runs it over the stumps of withered trees. She twines the graceful vine. A thousand arts she practices to animate and please the mind. Follow her example, and do for yourself what she is always laboring to do for you.—*Cotton.*

We are glad to make the above quotation, for it is not only a medical whisper, but rather a short sermon on love, which may prove the best remedy, after all, to heal many of our infirmities; the best medicine in our pharmacy we have, for perhaps you have lost the bright, fresh feelings of the soul.

But we would add, if the writer had only made a more comprehensive supposition (including all the married throughout the world), we could reply affirmatively; except, of course, all such ordinary broils—those which are always so indispensable as to meet the demands of honest hunger. Let the already truly married still keep up the practice of early courtship. Don't let the principles of Harmonial Love and wisdom ever become old and stale, and die out of your hearts, for it will always sound sweet to be again and again told that we are loved and appreciated by our conjugal companion; it always acts upon the soul like a tonic. No matter how tired and vexed and worn out with the duties of the day, it will always stimulate you to new strength and vigor. And let all those who are about to embark upon their conjugal existence regulate all of their attachments, and live by spiritual delicacy and private truthfulness. If all those who chance to read this prescription will try it, we feel we could guarantee that such a house would be a natural sanctuary of heavenly blessedness. The family circle would shine and sparkle like a ring of diamonds, and each throbbing heart would be a wellspring of love, tenderness, grace and gladness. All good angels would go in and out of such a sunny home, just exactly as the healthy children thereof would glide to and fro on the swift feet of unrestrained enjoyment.

A divine joy is certain to pavilion such a happy home, and one tender hand is sure to embrace all hearts which come within its influence, for it would be the very gates of heaven.

COURTSHIP AND MARRIAGE.

If we would have the nuptial union last,
Let reason be the link that holds it fast.

Courting, as usually conducted in what is considered the best society, is absolutely wrong. It places both parties in false and unnatural relations. It renders an actual knowledge with each other's inmost thoughts, feelings and desires difficult and unnatural. It can only be compared to a method of deception, in which each is trying to deceive the other. A young gentleman who is regarded as eligible, and a young lady considered of marriageable age, always put on their best clothes, their sweetest smiles and most winning ways in each other's presence, concealing the conduct of their real life. They seldom see each other as they really are; interviews are always formal; place and time announced; certain preparations made for them, so they shall not be seen without the customary disguise; and then, to increase the confusion, the young lady is taught not only to act falsely, but lie and deceive. Mothers teach their daughters that men should make all the advances; that it would be impropper for her to intimate a wish or desire until marriage is proposed, when she has the privilege of accepting or declining; that it is immodest in her to express a desire in regard to marriage, or for her to do any part of the courting is unladylike, while for her to propose to a man would be perfectly shocking. But no reason has ever been assigned why courting was not as much the right and duty of a woman as of a man, and no good reason ever will be given. There are many reasons why a woman has an equal right with man to choose a companion for life, one of which is, that she is as much of an indi-

vidual as he, and another, her peculiar intuitive nature making her more capable of deciding. But the
strongest reason of all is the function of maternity. As a rule, women could, if allowed by
society, select suitable husbands better than men
can select wives. It is too true that sensible young
girls marry very strange specimens of the opposite
sex, who are as uncongenial as December and May.
But what else can they do? They have been taught
that marriage is a necessity; that position and
wealth was of more importance than a love companion, and the result of such a union would be
followed by misery and unhappiness. How wisely
it has been said a truly mated pair in a hovel have
no reason to envy a couple who are married but
not mated dwelling in a palace. One of the greatest mistakes of the age is in separating the sexes
in their various vocations in life. They should
mingle freely and familiarly (of course under the
instruction of parents or guardians) at home, in
the field, work-shop, at school, and in social life,
as the association of each refines, energizes, and
enobles the other. If this plan were adopted they
would be free, frank and natural; each would have
a perfect understanding of the other's true feelings
and love making would not be done in the dark
nor on the sly, the happiness conferred by each on
the other being the sole occasion of love bound
together with the strongest band of union con-

nected with our nature. For the benefit of the young we can give no better description of what a true companion should be than copying the following poem:

CHOOSING A WIFE.

Enough of beauty to secure affection;
Enough of sprightliness to secure dejection,
Of modest diffidence to claim protection;
A docile mind, subservient to correction,
Yet stored with sense, with reason and reflection,
And every passion held in due subjection.
And faults enough to keep her from perfection.
When such I find, I'll make her my election.

CHOOSING A HUSBAND.

Of beauty, just enough to bear inspection;
Of candor, sense and wit, a good collection;
Enough of love for one who needs protection,
To scorn the words: I'll keep her in subjection;
Wisdom to keep him right in each direction;
Nor claim a weaker vessel's imperfection.
Should I e'er meet with such in my connection,
Let him propose, I'll offer no objection.

The first consideration in those contemplating marriage is to study each other's temperaments, to learn as much as possible whether their adaptations of soul element will blend together sufficiently to produce the most complete harmony, as it is intended for a life which should bring with it permanent happiness. For the sake of offspring and the nation, it is vastly more important that mothers should possess a more vigorous bodily constitution than the father, if either must be frail. But it is not necessary that every woman, to be a candidate for matrimony, should possess the precise features, nor the exact form, nor the full size, nor the balanced organism of the Venus de Medici. She may be taller or shorter, fuller or more slender, blonde or brunette, etc., but she must not be contracted around the lower portions of the chest; she must not be " wasp-waisted," concaved where she should be round, full, and convex. Such a woman cannot half breathe; she can neither feel, think, nor act normally. She cannot love, she cannot judge, she cannot do as a healthy woman would, nor is it possible for a man to love her in return, however tender and kind he may treat her, as he could and would one who could gratify not only one, nor several, but all of his mental powers. The woman should look well into all these essential qualities in choosing a husband. We have long since advocated woman's equality, mental and physical, and her equal rights, domestic, social, civil, political and religious. We cannot conceive of any right or privilege as relates to the individual, to the family circle, to society, or to government which man claims for himself, that woman may not justly claim for herself.

Rights no more pertain to sex than they do to nation or race; they inhere in humanity. If wo-

man is a human being and a fellow citizen, the
question is settled in her favor. If she is not, what
is she? If there are any laws which appropriate
her to man, they are man-made laws, not God-
given. Human statutes do not always "re-enact"
the higher law. Because in marriage the twain
become one flesh, it no more follows that the woman is to lose her individuality in society, and
her inherent rights before the law than the man
should lose his. They are, indeed, one in heart,
mind, life, purpose, but two persons nevertheless.
These are some of our ideas upon which the only
true basis of marriage can be entered upon with
any degree of permanent happiness. But marriage
of the present day is entered into altogether upon
a different plan; it is now governed by title, wealth
and position. And where wealth has little or no
influence parents often interfere to an unwarranted
extent, which many times blasts the hopes and happiness of a whole life. Now, when a marriage
takes place the almost invariable inquiry among
friends is, "Has she done well," which generally
signifies, has she married a house and lot, a good
supply of pretty furniture, or a large amount of
bank and railroad stock, or a comfortable pile of
money. This question is too universally regarded,
so much so that the respondent in reply begins at
once to tell how rich or poor the husband is. If a
wealthy position has been obtained by the bride,

the parents and friends congratulate themselves on the success of the daughter, and the unanimous exclamation is, "She has done so well." Young women in the highest circles often sell themselves to old men, double or triple their age, or are so sold by their parents, and do not seem to dream that they are bartering away their virginity and womanly charms for gold, the same, virtually, as the abandoned woman who walks the pavements of great cities. It is true that there may be cases where mutual love exists in such unequal copartnership, but they are rare exceptions. Wealth, rank, beauty and accomplishment are not, of course, to be despised—they have their value. But how contemptible it is that many, not to say most, of our best Christian families never give the young any other instruction with regard to courtship and marriage than what may be gathered from these mere externals. What one party or the other has gained or is likely to gain of personal beauty or pecuniary advantage will be far more likely to elicit attention in almost any social circle, either within the family pall or beyond it. The wife may mean while she aspires to learn all she can, not from novels, but from nature and works calculated to enrich the mind, and, in brief, of every source within her reach.

Now, is it at all unnatural that the progressive companion should, little by little, lose respect for the belittling qualities from the other? Then love exists with what finally develops into contempt, though the latter may not be unmixed with heart-felt pity. Just look how these people chafe each other continually. Can any good come of this domestic friction, which chips away as fine as iron filings the good temper and better qualities each possesses? Everybody is painfully conscious of the existence of evil, and this evil must be rooted out before the human family can settle down to a condition of peace and enjoyment. And so long as parents teach their children that "getting married" is all there is to life, they will be almost sure to acquire tastes, habits and manners which will unfit them for true soul companions. How often fathers give their daughters to fine homes, not husbands. Better for them and society that they were forever homeless. Let girls and boys be taught to know themselves, care for themselves, understand business, and let all schools, all libraries, reading rooms, all avocations, with equal wages for equal services, be alike open to both, then there will be no need of providing them with wives and husbands. They will find congenial companions and marry, or do the next best thing, remain unmarried. Surely there is no spectacle on earth which so demands our respect and admiration, and which is so suggestive of divinity and immortality, as an individual who, having fulfilled all the duties of

this life, is yet living in his purity and ripe old
age; one "whose eye is not dim, nor his natural
force abated, though whitened for the grave."
When one has lived a life in accordance with the
laws of life, they are not only happy in themselves,
but their influence is extended to all they come in
contact with. A lamp to the feet of youth and a
guide to the middle aged. And now, dear reader,
all I ask of you is, that, with a clear mind and a
pure heart, a love of the truth, and a willingness to
accept it, you read these pages, and so far as the
teachings they contain commend themselves to
your reason, that you follow them faithfully in a
life of purity and devotion to the highest good.
Doubtless, many things may be contrary to your
ideas of right. Humanity lies prone under the
errors of ages, and what we cherish as truths are
often the most hurtful of these errors. The only
mischief of error is, we accept it as truth. And
its strength is in the support of venerated authority. The miseries of mankind are but the
symptoms of its errors of thought and life. The
world to-day is cursed by error and discord, and it
must be saved by *truth* and *love*, a principle of
right and justice to all.

MOTHERHOOD.

This is a question which nearly all writers have evaded as harsh, untimely, or felt that it would not be accepted as modest; but we feel that the time has come when all people should put away such false modesty, and deal with the real facts as they are, and such important facts we all should know, and we must meet them sooner or later, whether we will or not.

Motherhood is the crowning glory of woman. But the ambition of the mother should be that of bringing the germ of able-bodied, great-hearted, glorious men and women, who will always be ready to do and dare for the sake of truth and humanity. The salvation of the human race all lies in the practical recognition of one important principle— one which, by future generations, if not now, in the light of our present science, must be pre-eminently acknowledged as an unquestionable truth, viz.: That she, who is the continued originator of the race, she, whose power and influence for weal or woe must be handed down through her posterity during all coming time, must be educated to, and shall be granted the inalienable, indisputable right to determine for herself when she can lovingly take upon herself the responsibilities of motherhood. The time has already come when

the mass of our thinking people have come to see
and know the one important, but hitherto neglected, lesson learned, that we are guilty of a hein-
ous crime, and one which nature never pardons,
when we will knowingly allow ourselves to become
the instruments of bringing into existence human
beings whose lives are a curse to the world and to
themselves, rather than a blessing.   Young men as
well as old must be educated up to this point, to
see the facts as they really are.

Till within a very short period physiology has
formed no part of the education of parents, and the
simplest elements of anatomy have been entirely
unknown to mothers.   Maidens have entered upon
the possibilities of maternity without the slightest
information regarding the structure of their bodies,
and still less of the powers of fœtal development
and intelligent understanding of the inevitable inquiries attending its arrest; and what is still more
ludicrous, were it not so very sad, ignorant even of
the conditions of parturition.   This, we claim, is
all wrong; besides there is no excuse for it.   We
must charge it upon an ignorant father and motherhood—motherhood not yet conscious of its high
duties, to instruct their children at least as far as
they know themselves, as well as to urge it upon
their children to seek for all the knowledge upon
these subjects that they can possibly avail themselves of.

It must be clear to every thinking mind, that it is not probable there will be any visible decrease in the crime of this world till the pulpit and the press, as well as the law-making power, are convinced that no persuasion, or education, or even punishment, or statutory enactments, can ever be made to cure those who are organically, morally, mentally or physically diseased. As the unborn individual cannot be consulted as to the character of his mind or his intellectual powers, he is, therefore, dependent upon the condition and the character, the intellectual and moral character of his immediate progenitors. Indeed, he has no more control over his moral or mental organization than he has over the color of his eyes or hair.

Our organization is *made for us and not by us.* Our present educational and religious institutions have not, and cannot, *prevent* the commission or increase of crime.

Why has not man sought out the means of developing and perfecting the human forms of his children as well as he has improved the stock of the animal kingdom below him? We do not .want passionless men, but men with strong passion, held resolutely under the check of an enlightened reason and conscientious individuality. It is high time that marriage should be regarded as something higher and nobler than a mere condition granting license to the passions. Let hu-

man beings enter into the marriage relation for the
sole purpose of companionship, for mutual improvement, and for the development of their own and
each other's noblest, best traits of character. Then,
when offspring is desired, let the prospective father
and mother seek to combine the very best advantages for the expression of their own and each
other's forces, so that their children shall enter
upon their earthly career with all of those excellen-
cies of physique and character that adorn the noblest
specimens of man or womanhood. The children of
such parents, conceived under such conditions, receive, at the moment of conception, an impetus
towards the good and the imperishable that no vicissitudes of life can ever obliterate. Such children will never fall into vice, but rather, as we see
them grow up to maturity, the very sight of such
noble specimens of men and women will be looked
upon and considered as the protecting arms thrown
out and around to embrace and protect the human
race. Happy are the parents whose children love
life and all of its opportunities. Happy are the
children whose parents derive the greatest joy
from their beautiful lives.

PREGNANCY.

Our object in speaking on this subject is to assist
the mother to understand her condition and relations to her offspring during this interesting period

(of gestation). How she may know when conception has taken place. She may have reason to believe herself pregnant when several circumstances combine to make it probable. First. If she has been exposed by sexual intercourse at the proper period, and the menstrual flow ceases from that time, followed by nausea in the morning, with unnatural likes and dislikes for persons and things; she may have sharp pain in the breasts, the areola around the nipple become darker, with pustule enlargement, perhaps difficulty in retaining her urine, and after a suitable time a gradual enlargement of the abdomen, becoming visible at the third or fourth month. If she feel the motion of the foetus at and after this period, there is pretty strong evidence of the fact of impregnation. And yet all these signs may exist without any certainty. The most unmistakable and reliable sign is the foetal heart-beat (or period of quickening), which may be heard from the fourth to the fifth month by placing the stethescope upon the mother's abdomen in the umbilical region. But some writers say, in speaking of the caution to be used in doubtful cases, never give a decided opinion until you have the child's head in your hand. All these symptoms and signs may exist from other causes, such as prolapsus, or other displacement of the uterus, ovarian trouble, irritation of the bladder, tumors, dropsy, etc., etc. It may be necessary to

call a physician to decide this question, when
strong feelings are awakened or great interest at
stake. The happiness of the mother may depend
upon his or her decision; hence the great necessity
of a careful investigation and a modest, frank reply,
with encouraging words to the fond, expectant
mother that the hope and ardent desire of her life
may be attained, the result of which will be a wel-
come little messenger from the holy bonds of matrimony. No mother should dread this happy ordeal, for, if rightly consummated, it is the highest
attainment a woman can know, and all the best
forces of both father and mother should be concentrated and put forth in this effort. The normal
period of pregnancy is from forty to fifty weeks, or
nine calendar months, counting from the last time
of menstruation. The time varies according to
the constitutional condition of the mother. If she
be of full habit, with strong vital force, the period of
gestation may be prolonged; on the other hand, if
she be weak and lack vitality, it is not unusual for
parturition to take place before the full term ex-
pires. There are cases on record where a six-
months child has lived; this is rare; but seven
months is considered the period of viability. Hence
the great necessity of the mother understanding
her true condition during this period, how to care
for herself and prepare the way for an easy birth,
as this is the next process she must encounter, and

with a proper knowledge of the laws of life carried into effect by actual practice, no mother will dread the pain of parturition, for if these laws be strictly adhered to pain is unnecessary. It was not intended woman should suffer, and it is only through her own violation that she does. Our aim is to give such instruction as will enable every mother who reads this book to look upon childbirth with pleasure rather than pain, for it is a natural process. The conditions required to accomplish this we will speak of under the head of Parturition.

PARTURITION.

The first thing requisite is a healthy, well-developed physical and mental condition. No woman should ever consent to become a mother unless these conditions be fully established, and no father should require or demand it. Conception should never take place without previous preparation and the full consent of both parents, under the best possible conditions. Much depends on the mother's influence. During the whole period her surroundings should be the most pleasant, her thoughts and feelings harmonious. This has much to do with the character of her offspring, and it should be the father's highest duty to grant and supply all these conditions. The mother should have plenty of *out-door exercise* from the first, not enough to tire her, but enough to keep the system active; wear loose clothing; live on the most simple, nutritious food—a diet composed largely of fruit is the best. Greasy food and pastries should not be indulged in at all. The body should be bathed in tepid water, with a little salt added, twice a week, a sitz-bath once a week until within six weeks of the expected time, then take one every night; the water should be of the temperature to make it pleasant and agreeable. Remain in each time from eight to ten minutes, then dry with a towel; when this is done bathe the lower abdomen with oil, rubbing it well with the hands. This should be done by the nurse or some friend. This course of treatment tends to relax the parts, and if followed closely will ensure the anxious mother a short and easy birth.

ABORTION.

Much might be said upon this subject, as the causes are varied and almost inexhaustible. Therefore, we will endeavor to speak only of the more common causes and their evil effects, making it so plain and simple in form that all may understand and profit by our teachings. The whole process is unnatural, and always attended with more or less danger, liable to produce serious and lasting results, and is one of the causes that entails suffering on our women of to-day, bringing misery and a life-long suffering of that most terrible of all diseases, female weakness. Among the most common causes is sexual excess during the period of pregnancy, and all parents allowing themselves to indulge in those relations do so with great risk, especially if the mother be constitutionally weak and the father violent in his sexual manifestations. There is danger in great sexual excitement of producing expulsion of the fœtus from the uterus, especially if it be near the period of usual menstruation. If this occur before the sixth month of antenatal life, it is called abortion; subsequent to this period, premature birth. No matter how it is produced, it is always followed with more or less unfavorable effects upon the general health, and frequently very dangerous, when accompanied with hemorrhage or other complications. Other causes may arise, such as fright, injury, or overwork; exertion of any kind, either mental or physical. But the use of drugs or instruments is the most prolific cause and the most unpardonable—a crime which will not be forgiven either in this life or the beautiful life beyond. The prevailing idea is, that no sin or crime is committed if it be perpetrated before the fœtus acquires vitality or individuality; or, in other words, the period of quickening. This is absurd, not the slightest physiological reason for

4

such an idea. From the moment of impregnation there is a gradual development of the life principle, both soul and body, and it should be remembered the whole period of gestation is a natural process, and should not be interfered with, but every part of it should be considered sacred, the highest aim in life sanctified by the holy passion of love, combined with the most exquisite sexual delight, to the grand, final result of the offspring being brought into existence, entering upon the great stage of active life an independent, individualized entity; hence the great wrong in destroying it.

CAUSE AND CURE OF FEMALE WEAK. NESS.

What mean these peace-destroying symptoms? Bearing down in the lower part of the abdomen, heat, dull pain, burning, weakness in the small of the back, sore place on the spine, small of the back so tender to the touch, dragging, aching in the loins, indisposition to bodily exercise, dread of walking—either far or fast, feeling wearied, numbness of the limbs. Why are our married women so capricious of temper, so childish, at times so given to transition from cold sensations to hot flashes; then from amiableness to peevishness, and fretful, with scrofulous swellings? Why are our children born with broken-down blood globules floating through their infant hearts? Why do their young bones absolutely ache with voluptuous fatigue, transmitted by ignorant parents?

Every ganglionic center is a telegraphic station; it receives impressions and transmits the signs and disturbances from point to point. Who wonders that our children are scrofulous, and so fond of sweets and stimulants? Who, that can trace the relation between one cause and another, will still grope around yet longer and ask the learned physician to explain why women are sick and unfit for ordinary duties of housekeeping? The pricipal cause of woman's suffering lies in Prolapsus Uteri (falling of the womb), Retroversions, Antiversion, and all other kinds of displacement; Whites (Leucorrhea), then inflammation and ulceration of the womb. These are the main causes which afflict three-fourths of the women of this country; yes, it is no use to attempt to disguise the fact that they are suffering, eking out a miserable existence, many of them without hope that there is any relief to be found for them, while many others, through false modesty, suffer and die in silence rather than consult a competent physician for relief; but, nevertheless, sooner or later the truth must be told that the main CAUSE of all of these reproductive diseases is caused originally by excessive and *unrestrained* indulgences of the animal inclinations, through ignorance. Neither man nor woman has comprehended the primal cause of their suffering; or what would be still worse—those, knowing the truth, will further practice the ungodly habit of intemperate reproduction. But, if you would be wise and strong, you should seek advice from intelligent persons, and reading books upon these subjects. Fathers and mothers should commence teaching their children, as early in life as they could understand, all they know themselves, as well as to surround them with useful books to read, that their children should not grow up in ignorance of the natural laws and functions of the organs of the human body, and their uses, as well as know the consequent suffering from their abuses. This subject is entirely too broad and deep for us to go into detail. This book is intended only to hint at the different subjects and point out the way you should do, and give such knowledge and treatment as is practicable, which will tend to relieve your immediate suffering and teach you how you can keep well, and prevent the suffering of others.

First of all we must give you our opinion, based upon twenty years' practice with female diseases, that the introduction and use of all kinds of Pessaries and Uterine Supporters have proved a failure to cure falling of the womb. They are not only useless, but they have proved to be very injurious. Now, the treatment we propose to give you is very

simple, but *radical* and *positive*. Every woman
suffering from these diseases should provide herself with a good soft rubber syringe—a No. 1 Davis
or Mattson's are the best. With this instrument,
properly used, she can cure herself of Whites
(Leucorrhea), and many other kinds of vaginal
irritations.

REMEDY No. 1.—Take the white of one egg, beat
it up well on a plate; after which add a tablespoonful of strained honey, thoroughly amalgamated; then add it to one pint of blood-warm water
and it is ready for use.

No. 2.—To one pint of warm water add five to
six drops of *diluted* sulphuric acid; mix well;
ready for use.

No. 3.—One pint of warm water, one teaspoonful of baking soda added; dissolve and mix well;
ready for use.

No. 4.—One quart of warm water; add one
teaspoonful of table salt; dissolve well; ready for
use.

No. 5.—One pint of warm water; add tablespoonful of ox-gall; mix; ready for use.

Nos. 6 and 7.—Make a decoction from the plantain leaf, which grows in your door yards in great
abundance, or a decoction from walnut leaves;
use a quart at one time, blood warm.

DIRECTIONS FOR USING THE SAME.—Where there
is much discharge from the vagina, you should first

cleanse the part with castile soap-suds, injected with
your syringe; after use Remedy No. 1, commencing in the morning; inject slowly, that the medicine may have a chance to affect all parts of
the vagina. At noon you can use No. 2, and at
bedtime use No. 3, in like manner. Use these
remedies for several days in succession, then you
can substitute either one of the other remedies,
and thus alternate them until you get well. In
the meantime take the following medicine internally; get your druggist to put it up:

> Fluid extract black cohosh............1 drachm.
> Fluid extract chamomile.............1   "
> Fluid extract of dandelion..............1 ounce.
> Glycerine sufficient to make a four-ounce mixture.
> DOSE.—Teaspoonful one hour after each meal.

This treatment persisted in will cure any ordinary case.

In cases of falling of the womb, or where there is
a little inflammation or ulceration, it can be cured
by the following medicine. Get your druggist to
put it up for you:

> Glycerine............................6 ounces.
> Tanic acid...........................½ ounce.

Mix by a gentle heat till the acid is all dissolved.
Take a tuft of fine cotton, about the size of a small
hulled walnut; after tucking the fringed edges
over to the center, take four stitches through the
tuft of cotton with a strong patent thread; soak

this tuft of cotton in the glycerine and tannin medicine. Just before going to bed, let some lady friend insert the cotton in the vagina as far as she can push it with the finger, leaving three or four inches of the thread hanging outside; let it remain until ten or eleven o'clock next day, then by the thread you can remove it. Then inject a little warm soap-suds, and cleanse the parts. This tanic acid mixture will stain your sheets or clothes; better prepare for it. This treatment, with the cotton tuft and glycerine medicine, can be kept up every evening, or every other day, or third day, as the nature of the case demands; from five to six applications are generally sufficient to effect a cure, by keeping up the other washes and injections between times.

This method of treatment and handling these diseases is simple and harmless, and perfectly reliable. The author has had no occasion to use any other remedies for many years. However, we might add, when there is much irritation, smarting or burning sensation in the walls of the vagina, it can soon be healed and cured, by beating the white of one egg, and add to a pint of warm water, to be used as an injection in place of one of the others.

HOMŒOPATHIC TREATMENT.

This dreaded disease that so many of our women are troubled with, requires close attention. Much depends on the dress, diet, etc.; in fact, all their habits of life. The clothing should be loose, hanging from the shoulders; the feet kept dry and warm; elastics should not be worn around the leg, the stockings should be supported from the waist, leaving room for free circulation to all parts of the body. The diet should be plain and nutritious, spices and greasy food should be avoided; fruit and grains should be generally indulged in; plenty of fresh air (which is nature's best remedy), and a salt-water bath twice a week; exercise enough to keep the system in action; with a happy, contented mind, and the addition of a few simple remedies, we think much of the suffering may be overcome. We fully agree with the above treatment in regard to dispensing with pessaries and supporters; they only prevent nature from doing its work instead of assisting it. For an external wash we will prescribe the Fluid Extract of Hydrastis; teaspoonful to a pint of tepid water; use as an injection twice a day. We also recommend the use of the tampon (or cotton tuft), after removing it take an injection of warm salt and water to cleanse the parts. Teaspoonful of salt to a pint of water.

Bell. 3.x.—Indication: Bearing down pains, as

if uterus would issue forth; profuse leucorrhea with severe headache, constipation or diarrhœa.

Calc. carb. 3.x.—Indication: Leucorrhea, with milk-like discharge during micturition (or urinating) too early and too profuse menstruation; walking produces great fatigue. Scrofulous diathesis. Ten drops of each in half tumbler of water. Dose, teaspoonful, alternate every hour.

Igna. 12.x.—Indication : Violent labor-like pains, with pressing in the region of the womb. Weak, empty feeling of the stomach. She seems full of suppressed grief. Difficult stool. Alternate this remedy withPuls. 3.x. Ten drops to half tumbler of water. Dose, teaspoonful every hour.

Sabina. 6.x.—Indications: Painful, active congestion of the uterus; thin yellowish leucorrhea; either suppression or profuse menstruation (in sluggish circulation it acts as a tonic); severe itching in the vagina, with drawing pains in the small of the back. Fifteen drops in half glass of water. Dose, teaspoonful every one, two, or three hours, as the case may require.

The Hypophosphite of Lime is an excellent uterine regulator, taken as a constitutional remedy, especially where profuse perspiration manifests itself in the axilla, groin, hands and feet. This remedy can be had at any drug store. The dose of the crude drug should be from one to three grains, two or three times per day; dissolve in water.

MENORRHAGIA (Profuse Menstruation).

This form of disease is characterized by profuse, prolonged, or too frequent menstruation, especially if it be accompanied by headache, hot skin, full pulse, weight in the back, hips, loins, and pelvis; the patient becomes bloodless and weak.

Cause.—It is occasioned by confinement to hot rooms, abortion, leucorrhea (whites), also excessive venery, long walks, and constipation. Exhaustion follows the least exercise.

Treatment.—Locally, injection of a decoction of the plantain leaf, alternated with golden seal (Hydrastis canad.), or a little salt and water; if the hemorrhage is very active, then a strong decoction of tannic acid, or, what is still better, a decoction from the bark of the red oak.

Internally, give the following:

Fluid extract of chamomilla,

Fluid extract of ergot,

Fluid extract of sweet bugle weed (lycopus), of each half a drachm;

Glycerine, four ounces.

Mix.

Dose, teaspoonful every two or three hours, as the case requires, and as improvement is noted prolong the intervals, and when the flow entirely ceases stop the medicine till the next period comes around; the local treatment should be kept up every day till the diseased condition is healed, after which the patient should have a tonic treatment to build up the lost physical forces. The following is called for:

Tonic Prescription.—Fluid extract of the tag alder (Alnus rubra),

Fluid extract of wahoo (Euonymus),

Fluid extract columbo root (Frasera car), of each half an ounce;

Carbonate of iron;

Hypophosphate of lime, of each one drachm;

Table salt, half a drachm;

Good sherry wine (or California angelica wine) and syrup of wild cherry, equal parts, sufficient to make an eight-ounce mixture.

Mix.

Dose, teaspoonful one hour after each meal, and on going to bed. We consider this one of the best general tonic medicines that was ever given in such cases. You can get your druggist to put it up for you.

These tinctures can always be had at the homœopathic pharmacies of a better quality than at any other drug store; but you must always call for the mother tincture.

HOMŒOPATHIC TREATMENT.

This condition should be followed by the same treatment spoken of under the title of female weakness. The general health looked after; then take internally the following remedies:

Bell. 3.x.—Indication : Profuse discharge of light red blood; flushed face, red eyes; full, bounding pulse, nausea, with rumbling in the abdomen; great weight from above downward; tremor all over the body; painful pressure over the sexual organs; pain in the back as if it would break; yawning, twitching and convulsive jerkings of the arms and fingers.

Cim. 2.x.—Indications: Discharge profuse, dark and coagulated, accompanied with heavy, pressing-down labor-like pain; nervousness, hysteric spasm, pains like those of rheumatism in the back and limbs. Ten drops of each remedy in a half glass of water. Dose, teaspoonful alternate every hour; continue until flooding ceases.

Apo. Can. 12.x.—Indication: Profuse menses, lasting from eight to ten days, with violent pressing pains; efforts to vomit; great prostration and trembling of the whole body, preceded for a few days by a moderate discharge; shreds or pieces of membrane come away with the blood; faint feeling; palpitation whenever she attempts to move; pulse feeble and quick. Ten drops in third of a glass of water. Dose, teaspoonful every one or two hours, as the case calls for.

Ustilago. Maidis. 3.x.—Indication: Copious hemorrhage during menses, with great restlessness and pain; *chronic uterine hemorrhages and passive congestion.* Slow and persistent oozing of dark blood with small clots. Fifteen drops in half glass water. Dose, teaspoonful every one or two hours, as the case requires.

DYSMENORRHEA (Fainful Menstruation).

Painful menstruation occurs mostly in single women.

Symptoms.—Restlessness, flushed face, pain in the head, back, and region of the pelvis, sometimes so severe that it will cause fainting; after a time the pain will become more bearing down, accompanied by shreddy mucous discharges and clots of blood. In young and plethoric persons there is but little effect upon the general health, but in very nervous persons the health soon fails, and they frequently run into consumption.

Remedies.—When it is thought to be persistent painful suppression, it is generally pretty certain that it is from an inflammation of the womb. Then the injections are called for, and the local treatment, as described on pages 53 and 56, under the article on " Cause and Cure of Female Weakness."

The use of mild cathartics is necessary to keep the bowels open and free, and the patient should take the following prescription:

Tincture of gelsemium,

Tincture of black cohosh (Cimicifuga racemosa),

Tincture of wild yam (Dioscorea villo), of each half a drachm;

Glycerine, four ounces.

Mix.

Dose, teaspoonful every three hours.

HOMŒOPATHIC TREATMENT.

First. Think of hygienic diet, perfect rest during the flow, elevate the foot of the bed; acid drinks, if desired; teaspoonful of salt to glass of water, patient sip frequently.

Local Treatment.—Be sure the rectum is evacuated if you have to use an enema (or injection); hot applications on the abdomen, either water and vinegar or alum and water; take hot sitz-bath every night until relieved. Take either of the following remedies, or alternate them; use the 3.x, and prepare in the usual way: Arsen., Bell., Cal. carb., China, Ferrum, Sepia, Cham., Hyos., Phos. Acid, Sabina, Lach., Sang. Either of these remedies is called for in all cases of this kind, and will relieve if persevered in.

SUPPRESSION OF MONTHLY PERIOD.

(AMENORRHEA).

This may occur in three forms: First, where the menses have never occurred; second, retention; third, cessation.

There are cases where the secretions have been perfect, but the discharge prevented by occlusion of the vagina, or imperfect hymen, etc. Again, the secretions may never have occurred, owing to a congenital deficiency of the ovaries. And there are other cases where the uterus and ovaries are sound, yet no flow from the vagina. The most common variety is when it ceases by degrees, as in consumptive and scrofulous patients; or it may occur as the result of cold, which induces inflammation of the uterus and ovaries. It may also be induced by excessive venery, or wet feet, ice-water, insufficient clothing, bathing, fear, grief, anxiety, falls, copulation during flow, or pregnancy.

SYMPTOMS.—Weight, pain in the head, loins and uterine region; hot skin, in some cases various hemorrhages, palpitation of the heart, chilliness, loss of appetite, etc.

TREATMENT.—Give hot alcohol baths, hot foot baths, if the suppression be recent; apply hot mustard poultices to the feet. Internally, give tansy or wintergreen teas. Keep the patient warm; get her into a sweat; allow but little exercise; give a hot sitz-bath, so as to concentrate the blood in the pelvis, putting the feet in a hot bath at the same time. Keep up this treatment for a few days, and all will be well.

HOMŒOPATHIC TREATMENT.

SUPPRESSION OF MENSES.—This is the most common form of amenorrhea; the menses, perhaps, may have appeared regularly for a short time, and become prematurely arrested while the flow is on. This is often the case; it may be caused from mental shock or some acute disease, exposure to damp weather; in other cases it ceases gradually, the flow appearing at the proper time, but becoming less and less each time, then disappearing entirely. Some constitutional disturbance is always the cause. The gradual falling off and then disappearing totally is the most serious, for it depends usually upon anemia, phthisis, Chlorsios, etc., etc. However, care should be taken in the diagnosis, so as not to mistake it for pregnancy.

The best remedies to meet these conditions are:

1. Asclep., Cal. carb., Cimicif., Helan., Puls., Sep., Sulph. sil., Arsen. These remedies may be taken separately or in alternation, if desired. Use the 3.x. Prepare in the usual way. Dose the same.

CESSATION OF THE MENSES.

This condition usually occurs between the ages of forty and fifty—sometimes later, sometimes earlier. The courses become irregular, staying away two or three months, then commencing with a perfect flood; then again coming scantily, just a show, with sometimes nausea and vomiting, bloating of the abdomen, tenderness of the breasts, etc., are the common symptoms. Pregnancy may sometimes be suspected, for there is frequent uterine pain, dragging-down pains in the back and loins, violent headache, sometimes vertigo, coated tongue and disordered stomach.

TREATMENT.—If the symptoms are light and this change is expected, keep the body in good condition by strict attention to hygiene, bathing and rubbing the body well three or four times a week. If the pains are in the lower part of the bowels occasionally wear a pack saturated with equal parts of whisky and water, with a little salt added. Internal treatment: Take eight or ten drops of the fluid extract of black cohosh three or four times a day. If the patient be weak and debilitated in general health, then the tonic medicine that we gave you in the other chapter is called for; in fact, every indication must be met in the constitutional symptoms.

5

HOMŒOPATHIC TREATMENT.

This is the most critical period of woman's life, and great care should be manifested in regard to her condition; if the general health be kept up the change will come and pass off with but little trouble; but if neglected, sorrow and suffering will be the result. A woman properly treated during this period should be as strong and vigorous as when a young girl. This can be done easily by a careful study of the laws of life and health. We will give a short list of remedies that will assist nature to do her work: Lach. 12.x. is the best remedy we have for hot flushes, 10 drops in half a glass of water. Dose, teaspoonful every one or two hours. Alternate this with Puls., prepared the same. Gels., Cal. carb., Ignitia., Bell. are also good remedies. Glonoin 3.x. Where congestion to the head in plethoric females, when the menses stop, fullness in the head, with or without redness in the face, throbbing in the head or pulsating pains, before, during, and after menses, or when the menses do not show themselves. 10 drops in half a glass of water. Dose, teaspoonful every hour.

MAXIMS.

1. Never eat a late supper and go to bed with a full stomach.
2. Never sleep with your hands over your head.

It impedes the circulation, and will produce heart disease.

3. Never bathe the head with *cold water*, but hot. for all diseases of the brain.

4. Human magnetism, the life principle, may be imparted from one to another, and is a very potent medicine in all diseases.

5. Sorrow, grief, fear or any other extraordinary emotion, *will cause disease.* So to be well you must be cheerful, and wear a pleasant countenance.

6. Never allow a child to sleep with an adult. There is an invisible magnetic atmosphere of sympathy emanating from and subsisting between individuals, which, if youth and maturity are brought into close conjunction, will always result in permanent injury to the youngest organization. It is a well ascertained fact that the *aged* will attract vigor and youthfulness from the young, therefore disease will always draw strength from the healthy, should the two continue to sleep together.

7. Never sleep upon any description of *feathers*, for they impart no life-giving element; but will always draw from you many of the atmospherical energies which emanate from and surround you at all times, and you will always rise in the morning tired and weary, without knowing that it was the feathers which had exhausted all your vital strength.

8. Never permit a sick and feverish person to wear the same garment, or repose between the same

sheets, longer than two days, because the positive disease of the patient, during the fever, is always absorbed by the contagious substances of the body.

9. You should never frighten, deceive or tell a lie to your child, because it is unnatural, besides very wicked.

10. Never love your child unrighteously. That is to say, never permit your love to smother your judgment nor blind the voice of reason, for you must know that sympathy (or love) is only serviceable when wisely bestowed.

11. It is more easy to manage and educate a child before its birth than it ever will be subsequent to that event, because the individualism is moulded, and consequently manufactured, more or less perfect in the mother's womb, because birth is before thinking.

12. Never make your child feel you to be its master, nor its inferior or superior, but an honorable associate. You should always substitute examples, truth and association for deception and lies, in your so-called family government.

13. You must learn to *will* and act, ere the child comes to live among you, as you would have the child will and act before the world.

14. The unborn child is a mirror, which will faithfully reflect all the wickedness and imperfections, or the goodness and righteousness, of its immediate progenitors. The era is nigh when all

the hidden vices, as well as the secret transgressions of both the ignorant and educated parents will be recognized and read in the face, form and character of their offspring.—*Davis*.

15. All nature, including human nature, is governed by immutable law.

16. All variation of character, physical and mental, takes place in fœtal life.

17. The compass and tone of each individual is absolutely decided before birth.

18. A marriage may be very imperfect, and the parties to it very imperfect characters, yet, through the influence of happily elevating conditions surrounding, and, as it were, pressing in on the mother, the children will be superior to both parents.

19. Education may modify, but never overrule, inherited defects.

20. Learn your child to do your will, and never decide without just foundation; or, should you hastily decide, never alter your decision without first explaining, to the comprehension of your child, your reason or reasons for so doing. But it is far better to have your child have perfect confidence in your wisdom.

CHILDREN'S DEPARTMENT.

A WORD ABOUT BABIES.

No house is complete without a baby; it is the well-spring of happiness. The young husband steps about with a dignified air, carries his head higher than ever before; he feels proud. Why shouldn't he? He is proud of the title of "father," and the fond wife looks and smiles through her tears, feeling and knowing that at last she has become a mother. Of course baby looks like papa, except its hair and eyes, they resemble its mother's, but no matter, it is a sweet little messenger, and the angel of the household. Next comes the query, What shall be done with it? Well, we will try and tell you, but first we must tell you what has too often been done. After being washed, its head must be rubbed with some spirits, then a cap is put on, then rough flannel next its little body, after this a host of unnecessary clothing to incumber it; then it must take a little something, for the little darling must be hungry—so a little whisky, salt and molasses are mixed and poured down its delicate little throat; next it must have physic—a little castor oil is given, then a little

(70)

baby-soup is mixed up and given, then it is put in bed to sleep. But, alas! it does not sleep, for here is where the music begins; the baby cries and frets, and no one in the house gets any peace.

But, surely, something must be done. I do wonder what ails it. Surely, it must be sick, says one; the child has colic, says another; then a dose of paregoric is given, in a few moments a dose of soothing syrup is poured down it, and baby swoons away under the influence of the narcotic poison it has taken; then the doctor is called. When he arrives he finds it in a fit that has been brought on by interfering with nature. All this is bitterly cruel, yes, an outrage; of course it was not done intentionally, but ignorance will not help the baby. This is no imaginary picture. We have known hundreds of such cases, and, as babies are not able to speak for themselves, please allow us to speak for them, and vindicate justice in their behalf. In the first place, no whisky, oil or salt is needed, but if they are all dispensed with you will soon see there is no necessity of either paregoric or soothing syrup, it will not be troubled with colic or spasms. No food is needed only what nature supplies from the mother. The baby will not suffer if it does not get anything to eat for the first twenty-four hours. No baby has ever yet died for want of food the first two days of its life; but there have been hundreds, yes, thousands killed, or their health ruined for life, by this unnatural treatment; if you do not abuse your baby from the first, its stomach will require nothing of the kind, it will sleep quietly and grow fat and beautiful each day. Its clothing should be plain and simple, just long enough to cover the feet nicely; if too long, will prevent the free action of the feet and legs. The clothes should be fastened with little tapes instead of pins; wash the baby with warm soft water and castile soap; a little oil may be needed on the head, under the arms, etc., to remove the gluey substance, then take clear water and rinse it off, dry with a soft linen cloth. When dressed, wrap in a small blanket and lay it in a warm, cozy nest, then you can sit down in peace and see it rest easy and sleep sweetly; this will soon convince you that you have done right. If the mother should fail to furnish the proper supply in three or four days, then you can give it artificial food properly prepared; take a little milk and warm water sweetened with sugar of milk; sometimes the mother's milk becomes impoverished, and, consequently, the child grows poor and is never satisfied; in such cases, as the child grows older it will require stronger food, and should at once be weaned; use a little bread, arrow root and sugar, simmer in a little water until it is quite smooth, then add milk until it is the proper thickness; sweeten a little and it is ready; another is gruel made from oatmeal well cooked; strain, then add a little milk and sugar; the nearer the food can be prepared like the mother's milk, the less injurious it is; remember babies are not always hungry when they cry; it may be a pin, the clothes too tight on some part of the body. Babies are like older people—creatures of habit—and it is wonderful how soon they form them. If you teach it to be rocked to sleep, it will cry until its desire is satisfied; so you see it is as easy to teach it good habits as well as bad ones. You can teach it cleanliness when very young with little trouble and regular attendance every day. Try it, and see; if you will, your baby will always be healthy, sweet and clean; and they are a joy and blessing in every home. All habits should begin from the first, then, instead of babies being a trouble, they will be a pleasure. The next process the little one is compelled to pass through is teething, and it requires careful and close attention from the mother or nurse. We cannot do better than quote from *Doctor Younkin's* admirable little pamphlet on teething, entitled, "A Good Nurse," with but little change:

TEETHING.

More children die passing this period of their lives than any other time; just when they have begun to grow interesting. Up to this period they have always been healthy; have not been sick a day; they are fat, and look so sweet; they have begun to pull on the love strings, which wind so tight about the mother's heart. But, ah, me; they are beginning to cut their teeth, and are so sick. Now, if we can be the means of teaching mothers how to save their children from the grave, while they are passing through this critical period of their lives, we will feel that this book has accomplished its purpose, and our life has not been lived in vain.

When a child is teething, there is a heavy pressure upon the gums from the teeth forcing their way through; this, of course, produces irritation and inflammation of the gums; they become very tender and sore to the touch. This acts upon the nervous system and is sometimes followed by high fever; the stomach and bowels are all out of order, and the child is fretful and sick. If the bowels become relaxed, and it vomits up its food, etc., do not fly to your soothing syrup, or your paregoric and laudanum. One drop of laudanum, or five drops of paregoric, or half a teaspoonful of soothing syrup have been known to kill an infant. Do not, we beg of you, suffer anybody to ever give your child these medicines, but use your little simple remedies which you know will do no harm.

If the mother fail to furnish sufficient milk for the child, or if it has begun to eat food, be careful what

you give it to eat.   Do not give it any green vegetables or green fruit, but resort to your Extract of
Beef, Oatmeal Water, Milk Punch, etc. (see pages
17, 20 and 22); they will be sufficient.   Keep the
child warmly clad; change its garments every time
the weather changes; if it is broken out with heat,
bathe its body occasionally with a little soda water
(such as you use for baking purposes), wipe dry and
dust its body with a little cream of tartar.   Occasionally give a little lime water in its milk; also
a piece of nice dried beef to suck—cut in a long
strip so it cannot swallow it.   If you follow these
rules, you will seldom need call a physician; but if
they should fail, you may call one who has experience in the treatment of little children.

When the teeth are coming through avoid
giving hard substances to bite upon, they break
the enamel upon the teeth and they are apt to decay.   The best thing is an India rubber ring.
Wash it clean, then spread some molasses on it, and
the child will work upon it with perfect pleasure and
safety.   But if the teeth are tedious in coming
through, and the gums become swollen and inflamed, you had better take it to the doctor and
have him cut the gums, or to a good dentist, who will
scarify them over each tooth.   We have done this
many times, and have been astonished to see how
quickly the stomach and bowel trouble would pass
away, and the child be apparently well in a few

days. When the child gets old enough to walk, do not make it stand too long at a time. If one child walks at a certain age, it·is no reason why another should. If you force it you run the risk of bending its limbs.

Some people are in the habit of frightening their children about "the doctor!" saying he will come and cut your ears off. He will pull your teeth out, etc., etc. This is all wrong. If you do not want it to be timid and a coward all through life, never allow anybody to scare it while young. How can the physician, under such circumstances, tell the condition of the tongue or the state of the pulse when the little one is almost frightened to death and trembling with fear? Do not terrify the child in this way. Impress them with the idea that when he comes he will cure them, and will be a friend to them when well; then the child will learn to be calm and trustful, besides much easier restored to health. When they have confidence the medicine has much better effect. There is a great difference between a grown person and a child when sick; an adult has a dread of death and the consequences after death. Hence, he submits very readily to treatment in the hope of living longer; while the child has no fear, for its mind is too young to be doctrinated into the false ideas of the condition of life beyond the grave. But the little one only dreads and knows its present pain. Children, therefore, if not too weak to bear it, should be amused with toys and pictures; give them a slate and pencil, a doll, pet dog or kitten, anything to cheer their little spirits and give the best chances for recovery.

CROUP.

Croup is an alarming disease, and requires immediate treatment in many cases to save life. Sometimes it runs a very rapid course and destroys life in a very few hours. We will tell you how it may be recognized. It commences with a short, dry cough, the cough always sounds hoarse; the breathing is increased and labored—there is a peculiar rasping, grating, or choking sound, which seems to proceed from the throat. If you have a case of this kind you should go to work immediately. Below we give you a reliable treatment that will do good service:

    Tincture of ipecac .... 1 drachm
    Tincture of lobelia seed 1   "
    Tincture of aconite root .... 10 drops.
    Powdered nitre..................... 4 drachms.
    Bromide of potassium............... 20 grains.
    Glycerine .... 4 ounces.
    Distilled water .... 1 ounce.

Mix together and shake well.

Take this prescription to your druggist and get him to prepare it for you; it will keep for years.

Put it in your medicine chest, as described on page 29. Have it marked plainly on the label, "For Croup. Dose, teaspoonful every half hour till relief, then prolong the intervals as the case may require." Now commence treatment promptly. Give a dose of the above medicine; make a poultice of bran, add some ground mustard, apply it to the breast and throat, and keep it there till it reddens the skin. Place the child's feet in hot water, adding hot water occasionally, till the child gets better and breathes easier. The author has saved the lives of hundreds of children by this treatment. It will not fail if taken in time. You should keep calm, not get frightened, and you will be astonished to see how soon your child will recover from these alarming symptoms.

HOMŒOPATHIC TREATMENT.

In addition to the above external treatment, if the poultice cannot be obtained quickly, use hot applications of salt and water, keeping the cloth covered with a dry towel, or, if preferred, rub the throat and chest with goose grease then cover with a hot flannel cloth.

Acon. 3.x.—High fever, dry skin, restlessness; child in agony, throws itself about; dry, short cough, but not wheezing; cough with loud breathing and great hoarseness.

Bell. 3.x.—Frequent barking, croupy cough, whistling breathing; hot, dry skin, face red, eyes congested, pupils dilated, tonsils red and swollen, great irritability.

Kali-brom. 3.x.—Spasmodic croup. Child awakens suddenly from a sound sleep by a sense of suffocation, with a peculiar ringing, dry, brassy cough and hurried breathing; child agitated, face flushed, eyes bloodshot, etc., etc.

Give the remedies as indicated or alternate.

Acon, and Bell.—10 drops in usual amount of water. Dose, teaspoonful every 10 or 15 minutes until relieved. If these remedies are not at hand, a syrup made from vinegar and white sugar, add a little alum; this is excellent and can always be had in every home; give while warm and every few moments, keeping the child as warm and quiet as possible, if it perspires so much the better.

WHOOPING-COUGH.

This disease does not show itself in two or three days, usually from nine days to two weeks. At first the symptoms are merely that of a slight cold; the child has a short, dry cough, particularly when food is taken; this will continue for a week, or perhaps longer, before you will notice any other particular symptoms. The fit of coughing is preceded by convulsive drawing of the breath, and, as it rushes into the lungs, causes

the peculiar Whoop; the cough lasts for a minute
or two, then generally ends with vomiting; the
breathing is then quiet for a time, and the child
is comparatively at ease until the next spasm
comes on. It is considered more dangerous for
children under two years old. If the child has
convulsive coughs, we would advise you to seek
medical advice. Medical progress has done much
toward a successful management of this disease,
the Eclectic in particular, to which class of practitioners the author feels proud to belong. They
have done much, of late years, by the use of newly
discovered remedies, to mitigate the suffering.
Many children are cured without going through
the usual prolonged time. But we feel we cannot .
give you special treatment for this complicated disease. It is not the purpose of this book to advise you
to handle medical agents of which you know nothing
about, but point out the true road for you to
gain your health. In mild cases, and with the
best care, the following medicine, red pepper tea
sweetened with honey, with a few drops of tincture
of lobelia, used as a gargle several times a day,
will be all that is necessary in most cases; but you
should protect the chest with suitable clothing and
keep the feet warm and dry. You must not resort to the usual cough medicines and syrups,
they will do no good and many times produce
injury.

HOMŒOPATHIC TREATMENT.

Acon. 3.x.—Indication: Constant febrile condition, cough dry, whistling, with soreness of the throat; the child grasps at its throat with every cough as if in great pain. Great restlessness and anxiety. Ten drops to half tumbler of water. Dose, teaspoonful every half hour until symptoms abate, then prolong the intervals.

Bell. 3.x.—Indication: Frequent paroxysms of coughing, worse in the night; barking like croup, face very red with every coughing spell, eyes swollen, bleeding at the nose. This should be given all through the disease, prepared as above and given every hour.

Kali. bic.—Violent rattling cough, with an effort to vomit; choking cough, with thick, stringy mucus. Alternate with the above, prepared and given the same.

MEASLES (RUBEOLA).

This disease is a continued infectious fever, preceded by sneezing, watering of the eyes and nose —a complete catarrh, accompanied by a crimson rash, and often attended or followed by inflammation of the mucous membranes of the organs of respiration.

SYMPTOMS.—After a period of incubation, vary-

6

ing from ten to fourteen days, there is lassitude, shivering, fever and catarrh. The conjunctiva, Schneiderian membrane, mucous membrane of the fauces, larynx, trachea and bronchi become much affected; swelling of the eyelids; suffused eyes, watery, intolerant to light; sneezing, dry cough, hoarseness, difficulty of breathing, drowsiness, and great heat of the skin; tendency to delirium; frequent hard, rapid pulse; tongue white. The eruption usually appears at the end of the third day; seldom earlier, often later. It consists of small circular dots or spots, like flea-bites, which gradually unite into blotches of a dirty-red color, and slightly raised above the skin. The rash first appears upon the forehead and face, then on the neck and breast, and gradually extends all over the body. It begins to fade away in the same way —first on the forehead, etc. It produces no marked desquamation, which is characteristic of scarlet fever. Diarrhea often sets in as the rash disappears. It is usually salutary. The fever does not subside on the disappearance of the eruptions, nor does the severity of the attack depend upon the quantity of the rash. The contagion of measles is active and varied. Pulmonary complications are apt to follow—laryngitis, cancerum oris, severe otitis, epistaxis, acute tuberculosis, etc.

TREATMENT.—Confine the patient to a warm, dry, airy apartment; enjoin thorough hygiene; have

the patient sponged off every two or three hours
with warm water or warm vinegar and water, then
give the

Tincture of aconite, 10 to 15 drops, in one-third
tumblerful of water. Mix.

Tincture of Belladonna, 10 to 15 drops.

Water, one-third tumblerful. Mix.

Dose, teaspooful; alternate them every hour.

Occasionally, between times, give warm saffron
tea or hot lemonade, plenty of it. Keep up, if
possible, a gentle sweat. Diet—milk, beef tea,
buttermilk and milk punch (see page 17 and 22).

HOMŒOPATHIC TREATMENT.

Aconite 3.x.—Indications: At the beginning,
when there is hot skin, full and quick pulse, and
much thirst, eyes red, watery, and sensitive to
light, with dry, hacking, or hoarse, croupy cough,
headache and vertigo on rising, 10 drops in usual
amount of water; alternate with Bell., prepared
the same. Dose, teaspoonful every half or one
hour, as the case demands.

Bry. 6.x.—Indications: When the eruption is
imperfectly developed, congestion of the chest,
shooting, stitching pains, increased by deep breathing; dry, painful cough, with roughness and dryness of the larynx; sitting up in the bed causes
nausea and faintness, thirst for large draughts of

water, 10 drops to half tumbler of water. Dose, teaspoonful every hour until patient is better.

Phos. 12.x.—Indications: If the disease be complicated with pneumonia, or if typhoid symptoms set in, tightness across the chest, with violent and exhausting cough, and rust-colored sputa, stitching pains in the chest, hoarseness, with loss of voice, 10 drops to half tumbler of water. Dose, tea spoonful every hour.

CHOLERA INFANTUM.

Sugar of milk......................half ounce.
Lactated pepsin...................35 grains.
Lactic acid ....
Hydrochloric acid..................
Aromatic syrup of rhubarb, of each..half drachm.
Tincture of prickly ash berries (xan-
thorylum).......................1 drachm.
Distilled water.....................one and a half ozs.
Syrup of lemon ....one and a half ozs.

Mix.

Dose, half teaspoonful every half hour, or hour, as the case may require. If it be too strong for the child, it can be made weak and palatable to the taste.

HOMŒOPATHIC TREATMENT.

Arsen. 3.x.—Diarrhea, vomiting, great thirst for cold water, but the drink is thrown off immediately; hot skin, great restlessness, stools dark and green, pale face, cold extremities.

Camph. 3.x.—Skin cold as marble, the child will not remain covered. There may be neither vomiting nor purging, only coldness and extreme prostration; rapid breathing.

Bapt. 3.x.—Very offensive diarrhea, day and night; child can swallow nothing but milk.

Iris. ver. 3.x.—Griping pain, diarrhea and vomiting of food, bile, or of very sour fluid; profuse, frequent, watery stools, or mushy, pappy stools, attended with discharges of fetid flatus; pale face, with blueness around the eyes, 10 drops in half a glass of water. Dose, teaspoonful every half hour or hour, as the case demands.

WORMS.

Worm troubles are not so common as is generally supposed. Almost every irritation or abnormal condition of a child is attributed by the parents or others to the presence of worms, and the little sufferer is often made worse by the use of medicines. In no case, however, should the child be purged and medicated for worms unless quite positive that such are present. Rarely do they exist without some evidence being shown in the discharges from the bowels; hence these should be carefully examined. Large sums of money are annually spent in this way. Get your druggist to prepare the following prescription:

Santonine......................................4 grains.
Sugar of milk...............................10 grains.

Mix and triturate, divide into six powders.

Give one of these powders three times per day for three days; then skip two days; afterward give the other powders in like manner. Pour it from the paper into the child's mouth—after which give the patient a sup of water. The child will not ob-ject. This is to be followed by a little salt and water. The child's food may contain an extra quantity of salt for a few days, but this excess of salt should be discontinued when it is rid of the worms. This is all the treatment any child need have.

HOMŒOPATHIC TREATMENT.

Bell. 3.x.—Symptoms: Flushed face and red eyes, violent starting and jumping during sleep, involuntary discharge of fæces and urine, gritting of the teeth, moaning and uneasy sleep, 10 drops in one-third of a glass of water. Dose, teaspoon-ful every hour.

Cina. 6.x.—Symptoms: Constant boring at the nose; frequent swallowing, as if something was in the throat; restless sleep, rolling of the eyes; short, hacking cough, particularly at night; abdomen hard and distended, with frequent pain in the um-bilical region; the urine turns milky after stand-ing a short time. Prepare as above. Dose the same. After these remedies have been taken a few days, take a few doses of sulphur 3.x., then return to either of the above remedies, as the symptoms indicate. All sweets should be avoided. A milk diet is the best.

CONVULSIONS OR FITS.

These conditions arise from many causes. Sometimes from teething, worms, or from hard, indigestible food that has been eaten—anything that will tend to irritate the stomach and bowels; or overloading the stomach may produce convulsions. There may be something wrong with the brain, or they may be produced from previous injury, a fall, or in some other way. But if the child be suffering from a fit, do not get frightened or excited; take things calmly, you can work faster when cool and deliberate, and to a good deal better advantage. *First*, seek the advice of your physician. If he is not at hand when the fit comes on take some cloths, dip them into hot mustard water and wrap the child's feet and lower part of the limbs, let them remain till the skin is quite red, and as soon as opportunity is offered give a teaspoonful of syrup of ipecac, or 20 drops of tincture of lobelia in a little sweetened water (each of which should always be kept in your medicine chest, see page 29), try and induce sickness at the stomach and vomiting, if possible. If the head should appear hot apply cold water. This is good treatment and will often bring the child out all right.

But when the doctor comes he will find out the cause, and prescribe for you accordingly.

OMŒOPATHIC TREATMENT.

When the little one is affected with this annoying complaint, little can be done at the time only to bring it out of the spasm. Then the cause should be ascertained and treated accordingly, whether it be constitutional or acquired. When the fit first appears the best thing to be done is to give a teaspoonful of salt and water, then put the feet and legs in hot water. As soon as the spasm has passed away give the following remedies: Bell. 3.x. Gels. 3x., 10 drops of each in half glass of water. Alternate every few moments until the little sufferer is better.

EARACHE.

First, the ear should be carefully examined to see if any foreign substance is in it, that may provoke the difficulty; if so, remove at once and it will bring relief. If nothing of the kind is discovered, we may know it to be the result of cold. Then proceed as follows:

Heat a brick or stone, wrapping it up with a damp cloth or towel, and place to the ear, heating and sweating it freely. At the same time take equal parts of sweet oil and glycerine, teaspoonful each, and add 10 drops of laudanum; mix well by warming it over the stove. Then take a straw or little stick, and drop 3 or 4 drops into the ear. This will give you relief at once.

HOMŒOPATHIC TREATMENT.

In connection with the above, we can only add constitutional treatment to remove the cause and prevent a recurrence, such as Cal. carb. 3.x., Silicia 6.x., Sulph. 30.x. These remedies should be taken separately in the usual way, continued for a week, then omit two weeks and repeat again. Continue this course until all symptoms are removed.

MISCELLANEOUS DISEASES.

LIVER COMPLAINT.

The liver is the largest gland in the body, weighing from three to four pounds. It is situated in the right hypochondriac, epigastric and a part of the left hypochrondriac region; the upper surface is convex, and in relation with the diaphragm; the under surface is concave, and in relation with the stomach, duodenum, hepatic flexure of the colen right kidney and supra-renal capsule. Its structure is composed of lobules connected by fine areolar tissue, and the ramification of the branches of the hepatic vessels. Each lobule is composed of cells, a plexus of ducts, branch of a vein and minute arteries. The minute ducts unite until they emerge from the lower surface in two trunks, which unite to form the hepatic duct. Into this the cystic duct from the gall-bladder enters, and the two form the ductus communis choledochus. The gall-bladder is a reservoir for the bile from the hepatic duct, it being full after a fast, and empty during digestion. The liver, then, is an assimilating organ. Its function is the secretion of bile, by which the hydrocarbonaceous portions of the effete matters from the blood are removed, as the effete, nitrogenous portions are removed by the kidneys. The bile, which is partly excrementious, exerts an important influence upon the process of digestion. It has an antiseptic action on the contents of the intestines. It stimulates the intestinal walls, and by a peculiar physical action on the fats and intestinal parieties, disintegrates the fats and moistens the villi, thus facilitating the absorption of the fatty matter. Therefore, this being the largest organ and one of the most important ones, it is very liable to become diseased, among which are enlargement, inflammation, acute and chronic, etc. This organ is more liable to suffer from depression than any other in the body, because it is more intimately connected with all other organs.

SYMPTOMS are pain in the head, with vertigo; mental depression, yellow conjunctiva; yellow, brown-coated tongue; nausea, vomiting, fetid breath, dyspeptic symptoms, pain in the right side and under the shoulder-blades, dullness at the apex of the right lung, caused by a depression of the eighth pair of nerves that supply the liver, which are reflected upon the upper part of this organ; there may be difficulty of lying on the left side; jaundice; there may be fever disturbance, with great depression, with inclination to sleep; great depression, loss of energy, indifference to life, sometimes diarrhea, but most always constipated condition of the bowels, with clay-colored stools.

TREATMENT must be very energetic if there be fever; the skin hot and dry, you must resort to the alcohol sweat-bath (see description of bath), or, if this be not at hand, then the sponge-bath must be resorted to, followed by vigorous rubbing with the towel. This is highly essential to secure a restoration of the cutaneous function; this treatment is of great importance. The diet should consist of articles rich in blood-making elements, with a rigid avoidance of carbonaceous food, fats, sugar, pastries and stimulants; plenty of out-door exercise, etc. The remedy best adapted to arouse the action of the liver is the following prescription:

Fluid extract leptandrin; fluid extract Euonymus (Wahoo), of each one drachm.

Fluid extract Podophyllum, five drops.

Aqua distilla, glycerine, of each two ounces.

Mix. Dose, teaspoonful every two hours.

Alternate the sponge bathing with diluted nitro-muriatic acid; acidulate the water just a little; the next time use common baking soda, table-spoonful to a bucket of water.

HOMŒOPATHIC TREATMENT.

Added to the above external treatment, when there is much pain in the region of the liver, immediate relief may be found in applying hot fomentations; this may be done by wringing a flannel cloth from water as hot as can be borne; let it remain for five minutes, then wet again; it would be much better to use two cloths and alternate them, having a dry towel to place over the flannel to keep the clothing dry; this is usually followed by relief in two hours.

INTERNAL TREATMENT.—Bry. 3.x. Burning, stitching pain, worse from motion; fullness of stomach and abdomen, pain in the right shoulder, yellowish face, white tongue, great thirst, constipation. Dose, 10 drops to half glass of water; teaspoonful every hour.

Leptandran. Hot, aching pains in the liver, with chilliness along the spine; yellow tongue; constant nausea, with vomiting of bile; loss of appetite. urine dark color, stools dark, dizziness, desponding, drowsy, with much soreness of head and eyeballs. This remedy may be alternated with Podoph. 12.x. Dose, 20 drops of Lep. to half glass of water; 10 drops of Podoph. to half glass of water. Teaspoonful every half hour; as symptoms abate prolong the interval.

DROPSY.

This is a disease too complicated to go into details of its history and causes, farther than to say it may become partial or general in its manifestations. The main cause is from the large venous trunk being compressed, or obliterated, so that the blood can no longer circulate through it, while the collateral vessels cannot be relieved; hence dropsical effusion is the result, and the effusion is in proportion to the size and importance of the vein obliterated or compressed. If, for instance, in the vena cava, or large vein in the abdomen, compression or any other obstacle should prevent the return of the blood, then the two lower intestines, as well as the scrotum, would become filled with water, or serum, and collections may perhaps take place in the abdomen. Then again, if this obstruction takes place at the very center of circulation, namely, the heart, the return of blood everywhere would become embarrassed; then the dropsical effusion would become general. A cold will often produce dropsy, also eruptive skin diseases, such as scarlet fever, or rheumatism, or it may result from degeneration of the kidneys, or from glandular enlargement of the liver, etc., etc. Albumen is always present in the urine in this disease. This can be discovered by boiling the urine in a small tube, the albumen becoming like the white of an egg boiled.

SYMPTOMS.—In the first stages, weakness and dyspepsia; the blood loses its red particles very rapidly, there is great suppression of urine. In the second stages the symptoms are a pallid, pasty complexion, and often a dry, hard skin; drowsiness, weakness, indigestion and frequent nausea; often retching the first thing in the morning, and often palpitation of the heart. The most characteristic symptom is, the patient is awakened several times during the night with a desire to urinate.

TREATMENT.—This is one of those harrassing complaints which physicians in family practice seldom have the patience to investigate and manage with sufficient care. The condition of the stomach, bowels and skin should have special attention. Free action of the skin should be had; in this way the kidneys are relieved, and thus the blood purified. Stimulating diuretics should not be used, but, to get up a free diuresis, resort at once to the hot air bath two or three times a week, followed by oiling the body well with goose grease or olive oil, rubbing it in well with the hands. A counter irritation should be made over the region of the kidneys

It is our confident belief that this grave disease can be cured in nearly every instance if not too far advanced. We know it from the success that has always attended our treatment. We will cheerfully and gladly attend any of the readers in the place where we are at work selling our book, who may have this disease. We will give you a prescription which has always given us the most happy results:

Fluid extract of unicorn root (Helonin),

Fluid extract of Indian hemp (Apocynum cannabinum), of each one-half ounce;

Glycerine sufficient to make a four-ounce mixture.

Mix.

Dose, teaspoonful every two or three hours, as the case demands. If the stomach is weak and will not tolerate the medicine without nausea, take less at a dose, and oftener.

HOMŒOPATHIC TREATMENT.

To the above treatment we will only add a few internal remedies.

Apis. mel. 3.x.—Indication: Scanty urine, sleeplessness, absence of thirst, stinging, burning pains in different parts of the body; dropsy of the chest, with a sense of suffocation; great soreness of the abdominal walls, cannot get breath except when sitting. Ten drops to a third of a tumbler water. Dose, teaspoonful every hour.

Arsen. 3.x.—Indication: Œdema of the lower extremities; skin, and particularly the face, looks pale, earthy; great debility and prostration, faint feeling from slight motion, tongue dry, great thirst, drinks but little at a time; suffocated spells, especially at night, when lying on the back; rapid respiration, skin cool, burning heat inside. Twelve drops to half tumbler of water. Dose, teaspoonful every half to one hour.

Dig. 6.x—For all kinds of dropsies, with difficult urination ; pale face, intermitting pulse ;
doughy swelling, which easily yields to the pressure
of the finger; cyanotic symptoms, with fainting;
when there are organic affections of the heart.
Twelve drops to half tumbler of water.   Dose, teaspoonful ever half to one hour.

KIDNEY DISEASE.

The kidneys are situated one in each lumbar region, behind the peritoneum, between the eleventh
rib and the crest of the ilium.   They are usually
surrounded with fat, and held in position by their
vessels.   The supra-renal capsules embrace the superior extremity.   Their length in the adult is
about four inches, breadth about two, and thickness
about one inch.   Their weight in the male is
about five ounces, in the female about four.   Their
substance is dense and firm, but fragile, and of a
deep red color.   It is composed of tubuli uriniferi,
blood vessels, nerves and lymphatics, with a granular substance containing granular cells.   The
kidneys are the secretory organs of the urine, which
is the waste portions of the system, and is separated by the kidneys and carried out of the system.
Therefore, the urine is a solution of excrementitious substances which represent the transformation

7

of the albuminous ingredients of the tissues; they are the refused product of waste brought down in the blood, and separated and discharged by the urinary organs as described above. There are so many complicated diseases connected with the urinary apparatus we cannot go into detail with all of them, but will only speak of some of the most common disturbances.

A depressed condition of the kidneys takes place from many causes; the excreting power of the organ becomes impaired many times from the effort made to excrete the poisonous matter in the blood during the process of malarial or other poisonous diseases, such as small-pox, etc., or any kind of drug poison. The greatest effort of nature during disease to eliminate the poison from the system is through the skin; if this fails the kidneys suffer; if the vitals are feeble, or fail to perform their part of the work, an extra amount of labor devolves upon the kidneys. In measles, erysipelas, and the long category of cutaneous diseases, we often have the kidneys performing an excessive amount of work, and the result will be inflammation or congestion. It may be produced by mechanical injury, from intemperance, or from cold and exposure to damp weather, starvation, etc., etc.

SYMPTOMS.—When it is the result of cold it is ushered in with rigors and chilliness, and flashes of heat, the febrile reaction preceding the occur-

rence of pain in the loins. When proceeding from
mechanical injury, irritating substances, from gout
or rheumatism, the first intimation of its appearance is an acute, pressing pain in the right or left
lumbar region; the pain is deep-seated and but little augmented by pressure, concussive motion of
the body increases the pain; the urine becomes
scanty; if both kidneys become affected the urine
almost entirely suppressed.

TREATMENT.—Perfect rest, dry cupping over the
loins, followed by hot fomentations; after this the
hot alcohol sweat-bath should be given (see description of bath); at the same time take the following
prescription:

Fluid extract Gelseminum, half drachm.

Fluid extract Eupatorium, Pur. (Queen of the
Meadow), one drachm.

Fluid extract Sanguinary Can. (blood root), 10
drops.

Glycerine and Aqua Distil., of each 2 ounces.
Mix.

Dose, teaspoonful every hour, as the symptoms
improve prolong the intervals.

HOMŒOPATHIC TREATMENT.

Added to the above external treatment we advise
the use of a compress; take a towel wet in salt and
water (tablespoonful to a quart), place it over the

region of the kidneys, well bound on with a dry cloth; let it remain all night, change it two or three times during the day; when changing rub briskly with the hands.

Acon. 3.x.—Indication: High fever, secretion of urine diminished, micturition difficult and painful; urine saturated or mixed with blood, consequence of exposure to cold.

Bell. 3.x.—10 drops each in a third of a glass of water. Dose, teaspoonful; alternate with the above every hour.

Berberis.—Indication: Burning and soreness in renal region; sharp pain in right kidney near the spine, extending into the bladder; stitching, cutting pains from the kidneys to bladder and urethra; the urine blood-red, speedily becoming turbid, depositing thick mucus and light red sediment.

Phos. 6.x.—Indication: Skin pale and Ænemic; frequent, watery diarrhea; in complication pneumonia, bronchial catarrh, etc. Alternate this with the above, 10 drops of each in half glass of water. Dose, teaspoonful every hour.

Canth. 3.x.—Indication: Paroxysmal cutting and burning pain in renal region, which is very sensitive to the slightest touch, attended with pain in the orifice of the urethra, with constant urging to urinate; only a few drops at a time and very painful, sometimes mixed with blood; high fever, pulse frequent and hard, constipation, stupor and numbness. Ten drops to half glass of water. Dose, teaspoonful every one or two hours.

DIABETES.

This is a real disease which many parents are wholly ignorant of, therefore many a poor child has been unmercifully whipped to break it from the habit of wetting the bed—this is cruel.

CAUSE.—Diabetes is an affection of the system dependent upon a disordered state of the digestive organs, with a defect of the assimilative functions, which is characterized by a condition of extreme nervous prostration, a morbid appetite for food and drink, and the secretion of a large quantity of glucose, or grape sugar. It is, properly speaking, a saccharine diathesis, for not only is the starch of the food converted into sugar, but, owing to the morbid condition of the liver, or the nerves which supply it, the liver only secretes, *per se*, saccharine elements.

The primary cause of diabetes consists, then, in a morbid condition of the digestive and assimilative organs, which favor the promotion of sugar from the starchy or farinaceous substances introduced into the alimentary canal, and its absorption into the blood and urine. But we cannot enter into details of the subject in this book.

TREATMENT.—A regular course of diatetics is of the first importance. A rigid and careful avoidance of all saccharine or starchy articles of food must be observed, and a liberal, nutritious diet must be adopted, consisting of beef, mutton, venison, fowls, game, fish, etc. If the patient can afford it, a sea voyage; if not, a salt-water sponge bath every day, with a brisk and vigorous rubbing with the hands. Bits of ice, to allay the intense, craving thirst, should be taken. Buttermilk is a good drink. [Right here we wish to say, before we forget it, that in all disorders, if the stomach will tolerate it, buttermilk is called for as a drink. It will allay thirst as well as water; besides there is a lactic acid in the buttermilk which is good for the stomach ; besides allaying thirst, it is a nutritious diet. The author always prescribes buttermilk in all acute as well as chronic diseases with the most happy and gratifying results.] The body should be well protected with flannels; plenty of exercise in the open air, but never to fatigue. Tonics and alteratives are the medicines in this disease. The best medicine to give is the diluted nitro-muriatic acid, half an ounce to one ounce of glycerine, tea-spoonful to a tumbler of water, to be used as a drink.

Tincture of nux vomica, four drops ; diluted phosphoric acid, eight drops, to half a tumbler of water. Dose, teaspoonful every hour for several days, making fresh every day.

Our treatment should all be directed to the head and nervous system, rather than the stomach.

For immediate control of the spasm of the sphincter muscles of the bladder in children who are wetting the bed every night, we will give you several remedies for this disease, as one remedy will not cure every case on account of the peculiar condition of the patient.

You can get at your druggist's Squibb's etherial tincture of ergot; give it in from five to ten-drop doses, three or four times per day in a little water. This is excellent in some cases.

Tincture of iodine, in one-drop doses, three or four times per day.

Tincture of belladonna, from three to five-drop doses, on going to bed.

Tincture of gelseminum, from eight to ten drops, on going to bed.

The two last remedies are to be given only on going to bed. One dose per day is all that is required.

HOMŒOPATHIC TREATMENT.

We agree with the above external treatment, diet, etc., and will only add a few of our best remedies, to be taken internally.

Helonias 3.x.—Indication: Unnatural languor, feeling of weakness and weight in region of kid-

neys, general weariness ; wakes every morning
with the lips, tongue, and fauces dry, and a bitter,
disagreeable taste in the mouth ; passes large
quantities of pale urine; pain, with lameness in
the back; numbness of the feet and legs, relieved
by motion; dull, gloomy, and irritable; profound
melancholy. Ten drops to half glass water. Dose,
teaspoonful every one or two hours.

Phos. 6.x.—Indication: (Glycosuria, with phthisis); urine profuse, pale or turbid whitish, like curdled
milk, with brick dust sediment.

Sulph. Acid. 3.x.—Indication: Lassitude, debility, despondency, dimness of mind and sight, itching over the whole body, stitches in hepatic region,
skin completely inactive, cold and dry; large quantities of sugar in urine.

· Tereb. 6.x.—Indication: Inability to concentrate
the mind; dull and languid, relieved by frequent
micturition; despondency, weary of life, obstruction
of sight, sunken features, lips cracked and slightly
bleeding, epistaxis (or nose bleed), tongue dry and
red, foul breath, hunger and thirst, sour eructations
and burning in the stomach, with frequent urination. Prepare each remedy and take as directed
in the above remedy.

GRAVEL.

Gravel may be defined to be the discharge of a gritty powder or sand, or of small calculi deposits passed off with the urine, occasioning pain and irritation of the kidneys, ureters, bladder and urethra. Gravel is present in the uric, phosphatic and oxalic acid diathesis of the individual. The most common of the three forms is the uric acid—averaging 80 per cent. of all the cases. All ages and both sexes are liable to be afflicted with this disease.

CAUSE.—Gravel is caused by a false assimilation of the solids and fluids of the body, unhealthy digestive organs, confined to the continued use of soft water or exclusive lime water for both cooking and drinking purposes. Of this, however, the author's opinion is formed from a very extended experience and observation of this disease. In cities, where the people cook and drink exclusively cistern water, is where we have found the most kidney and bladder diseases. We do not believe anybody should be confined to live exclusively on either soft or hard water for cooking or drinking purposes, but for health they should use both; if we should be compelled to choose one or the other for an exclusive use, we should choose the lime water rather than the usual cistern water; in fact, no cistern water is fit to use exclusively for drinking and cooking purposes, unless it has a good filter attached, and there are so few filters used that are fit for anything, so far as filtering out any of the organic matter, especially the usual rains that fall in summer, which people are most generally too apt to catch and save. The falling rains of summer are hardly fit for drinking purposes, as the air is always more or less filled with the carbonaceous and malarious poisons that arise from the earth's surface and fill the upper currents of air with its deadly poisons, and as water is one of our best known elements for the absorption of poisons, how can the rain, which falls through this atmosphere, help being filled, more or less, with this poison, which finds its way into cisterns for drinking purposes, to say nothing of the dirty roofs of houses, and the filthy gutters and water pipes, which are always in every case washed off and out from dashing rains. All this dirt and poison filth has taken up its quarters in the cistern, to be used by the human body. This is all wrong, for nobody can have permanent health living on this kind of water.

We will give you our plan for a filter, which we have tested to our perfect satisfaction, and know it to be the best ever in use. It is cheap and durable, never gets out of order, and we will not charge you anything extra for our patent.

When you build your cistern, build it just a little

larger than the usual size, especially at the top. Now build an eight-inch wall right through the center, from picked brick, pretty hard burnt, not too soft and shelly, but with nice, square, sharp edges. Lay this eight-inch center wall to the top of your cistern; it must be laid in mortar made from cement, the same as you use to plaster your cistern with. Strike the joints well; be sure there are no air holes through between the brick and mortar. Join the center wall to the wall on each side of your cistern. When you plaster it, leave the center wall unplastered, and when your cistern is done let the water pipes in on one side of the wall, and put your pump in on the other side. As your water runs in the cistern from the rains it will filter through this eight-inch brick wall, and you will have the purest water you ever drank, and it will always be pure and free from any organic matter. If you will be careful in the winter and spring to fill your cistern after a heavy rain, when the roof has had sufficient time to be washed off, you will always have nice, pure, clear water. All cisterns should be cleaned out once per year. This filter will never get out of order, and will last as long as your cistern will, and be just about as cheap. This filter can be added to old cisterns if you will alter the top and make it a little larger, so that any one can put down a ladder and clean it.

But, bless us! we did not intend to write an article upon cisterns and rain water; but here we have switched entirely off the track and told you how to build cisterns. But after all, it is as good a chapter as there is in the book, so we hope the reader will excuse us, while we try and find our way back to where we started from.

Let's see; we were trying to write an article upon the disease of gravel, weren't we?

But we will surely have to go back and read over what we said, and see where we left off, so that we can pick up the dropped thread, tie a knot, and go on.

Gravel, then, as we have said, is caused by an improper assimilation of the fluids of the body, which soon form into sand-like deposits. When the sediments are excessive they are called, chemically speaking, urates, lithates, phosphates, oxalates, according to the diathesis of the patient. When those assimilations are excessive it causes a serious disease, and if there is anything in the bladder like a mucous shred it acts as a nucleus for these sand-like deposits, and it forms what is known stone in the bladder.

SYMPTOMS.—In gravel, the patient has dull, aching pain in the back, preceded by and attended with frequent desire to urinate, followed by sharp, cutting, burning pains in the urethra and neck of the bladder, or in the course of the ureters. These pains extend along down the thigh and into the calves of the legs. The sudden stoppage of the stream of urine is caused by the stone rolling down into the neck of the bladder, and the patient has a constant desire to be pulling at the end of the penis to relieve the pain, which is always suggestive of the presence of stone in the bladder.

The chemical nature of gravel should be ascertained; when this is done, the chemical opposites in the medicines should be administered, as no treatment will avail if not in chemical opposition. But if the stone has been formed, and is of any size, there is no treatment effectual. A surgeon should be consulted, who will remove it by an operation called lithotrity, or another term, lithontripsy.

The solvent treatment consists of such agents as are chemically opposed to the nature of the calculi deposits. By such a course of medication our success has been the most gratifying.

As soon as the patient is aware or has the least suspicion he has the gravel, he should at once see that his stomach, as well as all the internal organs, are in good running order. A strict nutritious diet should be adhered to. Sponging and bathing is in order and loudly called for. All stimulating drinks should be avoided, and adopt the mucilaginous drinks.

Then the following prescription is a specific to neutralize and get rid of the sand-like deposits.

The best remedy we have ever used is a tincture made from the inner bark from the root of the sweet apple tree. The medical properties are only in the root late in the fall and early in the spring, before the sap rises up in the tree, and after it has gone down into the roots. You can make it yourself in the following way, as it can seldom be found in the drug.stores.

Take of the bark of the root, eight ounces by weight.

Put this into a bottle.

Add alcohol 76 per cent., one pint by measure.

Let it stand from fifteen to twenty days, shaking it occasionally that the strength be well drawn out.

Dose of this medicine: One teaspoonful three or four times per day. It can be taken in a little sweetened water.

The next best remedy is the

Fluid extract of hydrangea.

Dose, fifteen to twenty drops every three hours.

Ten grains of borax dissolved in water should be drank every day during the treatment.

HOMŒOPATHIC TREATMENT.

This disease is very difficult to manage, and has baffled the skill of all schools, and the treatment to a large extent has proven to be unsatisfactory, and where allowed to become chronic, the only permanent relief will be a resort to surgery.   The best way to avoid this disease, by its not being heredit- ary, is to pay close attention to the general health. When the calculi has already formed, the most di- rect way of treating is to inject the medicine into the bladder, thus dissolving the deposit more rap- idly and effectually.   Any of the remedies men- tioned may be used; quantity small, teaspoonful to a cup of tepid water.

The following list are the remedies called for; prepare and take in the usual way: Berberis 2.x., Phos. 6.x., Eupat. purp., Urva. ursi 1.x., Sil. 3.x., Zinc 6.x., Amm. arn. 3.x., Borax crudun, Nux mosch. 3.x., Sep. 3.x., Bell. 3.x., Canth. 3.x., China 3.x., Cal. carb. 6.x.

INFECTIOUS DISEASES.

These are propagated by a specific contagion, which gains access to the blood, thereby generat- ing a virus in the system.   They are contracted by inhalation of gaseous exhalations, patients suffer- ing from diseases, or the discharged materials from the lungs, skin, or bowels.   The atmosphere in neighborhoods may be so impregnated with this poison as to cause what is known an EPIDEMIC.

When a quantity of contagious matter, however small, is introduced into the blood of a healthy person, it will be propagated into the blood, and disease is the result. You should never undertake the treatment of these diseases yourself; better employ a good physician and a good nurse, then you have done the best possible thing. When the skin begins to peel off, if it is a child, you will find it constantly picking at the nose, lips, teeth, or finger-nails. It is a curious fact, how they will interest themselves for hours, picking at themselves till they bleed, without seeming to feel the least pain; nor is it any use to find fault with them, or even threaten them, it will do no good; it seems to be a part of the disease. Your only remedy is to place mittens upon the hands. After scarlet fever or small-pox, the room, with all its furniture, should be thoroughly disinfected. To accomplish this, cleanse the floor with hot water and lime, or carbolic acid; close the room air-tight, after removing everything from it, and then burn flour of sulphur; this can be done by placing an iron kettle, with legs to it, in the center of the room. Or, better still, heat the kettle sufficiently hot to burn sulphur, then sprinkle two or three ounces of sulphur in the kettle, hasten out and close the door tight; let this remain closed for three or four hours, then it can be opened and aired for several days; if you should whitewash the walls, your room would be as pure as ever.

SMALL-POX (VARIOLA.).

This disease is too well known to need a particular description. It is always caused or communicated by contagion; that is, caught from others who have it. There are two forms—the confluent, when the vesicles are so thick that they run together; and distinct, when they are separate. Then we have small-pox, or varioloid, modified by constitutional predisposition—we won't say by vaccination, because we don't believe vaccination ever prevented a case of small-pox; but, on the contrary, we know of many cases of confluent small-pox after the patients informed us they had been vaccinated and took well. Therefore, we would advise you never allow your children to be vaccinated under any consideration. Our own observation in regard to the human family we have formed after an experience of over twenty years in the practice of medicine, and have long since arrived at the conclusion that the inhuman practice of vaccination has caused more deaths than the disease ever did, to say nothing of the consumptive and scrofulistic wrecks that vaccination has left all over the world. From conscientious scruples, the author has never yet vaccinated a single individual, and we don't intend to commence now. Our voice shall ever be heard in condemnation of that inhuman practice.

8

If the rules and laws of health are observed, which we have endeavored to give you in this book, you need never be any more afraid of small-pox than any other disease. However, we will tell you the treatment in this disease is simple and easy to manage. We have a remedy from London which rivals all others for its simplicity, and, coming as it does so highly recommended, we apprehend that it has accomplished all that is claimed for it:

Dissolve one ounce of cream of tartar in one pint of boiling water. Of this, when cold, give half a gill for the first dose, to an adult. After this is taken, divide the remaining quantity into such doses as, taken three times a day, the whole will last three days.

It is said that this simple remedy has restored thousands of cases, and will effectually cure this disease in five or six days, leaving no pit marks and no blindness, as is sometimes the case when otherwise treated, and always prevents the tedious lingering of convalescence; besides, it can be taken at any time, being preventive as well as curative. The use of it is so effectual that, were it popularly employed, it would dispense with the unnatural law of vaccination and the very costly staff of vaccinators.

Another remedy, more in use in some parts of Europe, and also in China, said to be the most successful ever employed in those countries, and perfectly effectual: Apply to the chest an ointment made by combining tartar emetic and croton oil with lard. This application should be made when the fever is at its height and just before the eruptions appear. This causes all the eruptions to appear on this part of the body, and thus relieves the internal organs and the face, on which there will be no pitting.

HOMŒOPATHIC TREATMENT.

This is a rare disease, and dreaded by all when prevailing as an epidemic. Great care and attention should be paid to the sanitary condition. If a physician can be had, no one should try to treat it themselves, but in case one cannot be reached, we will give you the best treatment our experience has taught us. To prevent pitting: As soon as the pustules begin to appear, take a piece of cotton cloth the size of the face, cut holes for the eyes, nose and mouth; keep this constantly wet with diluted carbolic acid; this will prevent the air from coming in contact with the face, also the itching and scratching; if the vesicles are not interfered with, no marks will be left. The room should be kept somewhat darkened, but well ventilated; strict attention to diet, and give the following remedies as indicated:

For heat, burning and dryness, Apis. 3.x.
Alternate chill and fever, Acon. 3.x
Chest symptoms, Bry. Phos. Gels. 3.x.
Cerebral (or head) affections, Bell. Bry. 3.x.
Hemorrhage, Phos. 3.x.
Typhoid symptoms, Phos. acid 6.x., Bry. Rhus
3 x.
For rattling in the throat, Tartar emetic 3.x.
Collapse, or sinking, Carb. veg. Arsen. Lach. 6.x.
Retention of eruptions, Cham. 6.x.
Suppurative stage, Hep. Sulph. 3.x.
For inflammation of the lungs and trachea, Hydrastis 3.x.

Prepare in the usual way, 10 drops in half glass of water. Dose, teaspoonful every half or one hour, according to the severity of the case.

DIPHTHERIA.

Diphtheria is scarcely more than a modification of scarlet fever. The patient first complains of lassitude, aches all over, especially in the back and hips; headache, loss of appetite, rigors and chills, active and quick pulse, a light-furred tongue, redness in the back of the mouth, enlargement of the glands about the neck, a hot, dry skin, and in most cases an exudation formed upon the mucous surfaces of the upper air passages. This soon becomes or-

ganized into a tough, white membrane, covering
the soft palate and tonsils. These sometimes de-
generate into ulcers. The breathing, in consequence of the condition of the membranes and air
passages, becomes hurried and labored, and the
patient becomes very restless and uneasy, pulse
quick and frequent, the asphyxia ensuing ends in
death. The breath becomes fetid. No one, after
inhaling the breath and exudations arising from a
diphtheric patient, can ever mistake this disease. It
generally rages as an epidemic, and is regarded as
contagious.

TREATMENT.—The first step in the treatment
should be an emetic by a copious draught of milk-
warm water with a little salt and ground mustard
added. This should be drank slowly and continually until the patient vomits. No danger, don't
be afraid of too much water; it is harmless. The
vomiting will, at the same time, produce free perspiration, which is highly necessary, and should be
kept up by the use of the tincture of gelseminum
and aconite root, of each 20 drops, added to a half
tumbler of water.

Dose, teaspoonful every hour.

The kidneys should be kept in vigorous operation. Flannel cloths should be wet with the compound tincture of capsium, myrrh and lobelia, and
should be changed every half hour, and applied as
hot as the patient can bear it. till the disease is

under control, taking care that the throat is well protected from the cold air after the hot flannel cloths are abandoned. The patient should be kept in bed with hot jugs to the feet, and a gentle perspiration kept up. The bowels should be evacuated by injections of warm water.

The following prescription the author has found to be a specific treatment to kill the ulcers and exudations that gather upon the tonsils and mucous membranes in the throat:

> Chlorate of potassium_____1 drachm.
> Fluid extract wild yam (diascora villosa)__½ drachm.
> Hydrate of chloral_____1 drachm.
> Tincture of muriate of iron_____1 drachm.
> Carbolic acid_____5 drops.
> Glycerine_____3 ounces.

Mix well.

Get your druggist to put this prescription up for you. Then, with a camel-hair brush, touch the tonsils and all the exudations in the throat three or four times per day. If the patient swallows a little it will do no harm. If the medicine be a little too strong, it can be reduced with water. You will be astonished to see how soon the ulcers will clean off and begin to heal up under this treatment.

Give the patient plenty of milk punch (see page 22 how to make it). Add plenty of brandy, as it is said, by late observers, that good whisky or brandy is a prophylactic in diphtheria, hence you can add more than usual. Also give the extract of beef (see page 17). In convalescing, the patient should have a good sponge-bath every day, followed by brisk rubbing with the hands by the nurse or some genial friend.

HOMŒOPATHIC TREATMENT.

Much might be said about this fearful disease, but time and space forbid, and we think it very necessary that a physician should be consulted in all severe cases, from the fact of the results apt to follow; but with care and thoughtfulness on the part of the parent, or nurse, much suffering can be avoided. If a physician cannot be had begin with your home treatment; give the following remedies:

Indications: For dry, hot skin, very quick pulse, dark redness of fauces (or throat), Acon. 3.x. For great debility from the beginning, the membrane assumes at once a dirty grayish color; puffiness around the eyes, with pain in the ears when swallowing; itching, stinging eruptions on the skin, numbness of feet and hands, Apis. 3.x. For great dryness of the throat, tonsils bright red and swollen, swallows with great difficulty, very restless; drowsy, but cannot sleep; starts from sleep, jumps up suddenly; congestion to the head, with sudden pain, Bell. 3.x. With dark membrane in throat, offensive breath, dry, brown tongue, little or no thirst, oppressed breathing from pulmonary congestion, throat feels sore and contracted, prostration, chilliness of lower limbs and back, with hot face, fever at night, Baptisia 1.x. For large yellow deposits all around the *posterior walls of the pharynx*, which is ulcerated and sloughing; very quick pulse, flashes of heat, frequent sinking spells, dryness of throat, slowly progressing cases, Sulph. 2.x. For ulceration of throat, with large exudations, thick, grayish, or yellowish, sticky and tenacious; swallowing very difficult, liquids run out of the nose, excessive paleness, Sulph. acid 3.x. Prepare in the usual way, take according to severity of case, and continue until relieved.

ERYSIPELAS (ST. ANTHONY'S FIRE).

CAUSE.—Exposure to cold, impaired digestion, wounds, particularly from dissecting and surgical instruments; badly ventilated and over-crowded apartments, certain conditions of the atmosphere and a morbid state of the blood from disease, the habitual use of stimulants, etc., and consequently debility. The tendency of the disease is to attack different parts of the body simultaneously, which furnishes us with evidence of its origin in a bad condition of the blood. The chief existing cause of erysipelas is a recent wound, and the predisposing cause is inattention to the laws of health, combined, perhaps, with a personal or family tendency to the disease. Erysipelas is known by its inflammatory redness of the skin and its rapid tendency of spreading over the body, with considerable puffy swelling, tenderness, painful burning, tingling and tension. The color varies from a faint red to a dark red or purplish color, becoming white under pressure, but returning to its former color on the removal of the pressure. An attack is usually ushered in with shivering, languor, headache and nausea, bilious vomiting with the ordinary symptoms of inflammatory fever, accompanied or followed by inflammation of the parts affected. When erysipelas attacks the face, it nearly always commences at the side of the nose near the angle of the eye.

REMEDIES AND TREATMENT.—Applications, externally used, should always be put on warm, whatever form the disease may assume; cold applications should never be made, as they interfere with the free circulation of the blood and the nutrition of the part; and they always increase rather than diminish the extent of the severity.

There are many kinds of treatment, but we will give only those adopted by the author, which, in every case, have proved to be the most successful.

A poultice made from cranberries, stewed and cooked in the usual way, applied blood-warm, is a very valuable remedy for outward application. If

these are out of season, the next best remedy is a
decoction of strong tea made from the inner bark
of the burr-oak tree; use this to make a bread poultice, and apply it.   Also the sulphite of soda, half
an ounce to a pint of tepid rain-water; dissolve
well.   A cotton cloth wet in this and laid over the
affected part, one thickness, and kept wet by changing.   The cloth should be thoroughly washed in
clean water before putting it back in the soda water.
Also hamamelis (the witch-hazel) used in the
same way as the soda solution; use full strength.
Then again, I have used a gill of good brandy
with the juice of two lemons added.   Keep the affected parts well moistened with either of the remedies till the inflammation is well subdued.   We
have always been successful with these remedies
used in this way.   Sometimes we alternate two of
these until the inflammatory action is entirely under control.

But this disease must be taken in time.   It will
not do to postpone the treatment for one moment,
as it is very dangerous.

For the internal treatment we use the following
prescription:

Muriate tincture of iron..............3 drachms.
Diluted carbolic acid ....¼ drachm.
Fluid ext. baptisia – tinctoria (wild
      indigo).........................1 drachm.
Glycerine sufficient to make a four-ounce mixture.

Dose, teaspoonful every two hours.

If it is facial erysipelas, with much fever, it should be controlled by the mother tincture of belladonna and aconite. They can be procured at the homœopathic pharmacy. Give 10 drops of each in a half-tumbler of water; mix well.

Dose, teaspoonful every hour if the fever be high, and the iron mixture every three hours, till the fever is controlled.

Keep the bowels open by injections of salt and water, as described in other pages of this book. This treatment will do good service.

HOMŒOPATHIC TREATMENT.

We accept the above external treatment and will only add a few remedies to be taken internally. When the left side of the face is affected, painful when laughing, with sensation as if covered with a cobweb, Borax 1.x.

Chronic disposition of the disease to return, from right to left; phlegmonous of head and face, with burning, tingling pains; swelling and induration of lymphatic glands, very liable to take cold from the least exposure, Graph. 2.x.

For extreme tenderness and painfulness on pressure, with tendency to the formation of serum, the swelling hot, hard, shining, even deep red; patient feels nervous, cannot stand pain; feels tired as after hard work or as if beaten.

Arn. 3.x.—(This remedy is excellent for external applications.) For itching all over, especially on hairy parts after scratching; burning, swelling and redness of the face, with partial or entire closure of the eyelids; bruised feeling in the limbs and back, tendency to attack the brain, dark redness of the parts. Prepare as before stated, and give according to symptoms; as the patient is relieved prolong the intervals.

DYSENTERY OR BLOODY FLUX.

This distressing disease, of all others, may be controlled and cured by very simple methods, if not let run too long, till it becomes chronic. The first thing to be done in diarrhea is to stop all kinds of food, except the beef extract, milk punch, oatmeal water and mush, as described on pages 17, 19, 20 and 22. Slippery elm, or flax-seed tea made from the water off oatmeal, used as injections after each evacuation from the bowels, are not to be *omitted*. About two tablespoonfuls at a time, or as much as can be retained for a while. Bilious persons, having the obstinate form of this disease, will find great virtue in the following prescription:

Turkey rhubarb and willow charcoal (pulverized), of each one tablespoonful.

Of saleratus, a piece as large as a hazel-nut.

(The charcoal, put up in bottles, can be had at the drug store.

The hydrastis (golden seal), half a teaspoonful.

Add these ingredients to a tumblerful of water, stir well; let it stand covered twelve hours; after thoroughly stirring it, the liquid will be ready for use.

Dose, teaspoonful every four hours during the day.

Always remember this, never wake the patient to take medicine. Sleep will do more good than any medicine can. We cannot impress upon you too strongly the value of *magnetism*. In restoring health to the system, not only in this, but every disease, especially in stomach and bowel troubles, the *will* is a very powerful physician. Therefore, do not fail to avail yourself of his skill and beneficence. Always keep the feet warm and dry. Always sleep with your mouth closed, that the air may pass through the nostrils into the lungs, making it more pure and *magnetic*, therefore more energizing to the system, and thank the Universal God of Nature that in Him you " live, move and have a being," and your face will soon shine with gladness, your cheeks will blush with intensified vigor.

HOMŒOPATHIC TREATMENT.

This disease is very annoying both to patient and physician, hence it requires the greatest care.

The surroundings should be considered; everything obnoxious removed; pure air and perfect rest are the best remedies; prompt removal of all evacuations; use carbolic acid or other disinfectants; light diet is best—cream, mutton broth, gruel made from the different grains, toast water; nice ripe fruit is not injurious. Use the following: Rem. Acon. 3.x. Chill and fever, 12 to 15 drops in half glass of water; give every 30 minutes. Merc. corr.; 6.x. Autumnal dysentery cool nights, excoriating discharges, burning pain, green slime and blood. Aloes 3.x. Hemorrhoids, violent tenesmus, fullness of abdomen, pain both before and after stool. Give as above. Bry. 3.x. If pain be worse on motion, prepare the same, take every hour. Collonsynthis 6.x. Colic pains, with stools like beef washings, bitter taste in the mouth, great desire for cold drink; give same. Ham. 3.x. Blood copious in the discharge, very dark red; prepare same and take every hour. Sulph. 6.x. Chronic, bloody stool; take every hour. Ipecac 3.x. Nausea and vomiting, brought on by eating green fruit; prepare and give same.

DIARRHEA.

Bowel complaint occurs every summer, and often proves fatal to young children. It has been thought eating fruits was the cause, as it generally occurs at the time fruits are ripening and being gathered. But we think ripe fruit, if perfectly sound and fresh, will do no harm in most cases; while we believe that half-ripe or decayed fruits or vegetables are very unwholesome, and little better than poison. It requires good judgment to manage successfully all diseases of this kind, and no person, ignorant of medicine, should ever tamper with the life of a child by experimenting. Neither should they delay, with the hope of the child getting well itself. Delays and ignorance in the management of such diseases have been the cause of many deaths. In many cases, where it is allowed to run too long, very serious complications manifest themselves and are not easily controlled. But it is your duty to commence at once with proper food and simple remedies, such as described on pages 19, 20 and 21. This will do no harm, and many times will cure the case in two or three days. But if there be no change in that time, you should consult your physician at once; he will tell you the treatment was good, and will not order you to change the diet.

HOMŒOPATHIC TREATMENT.

This is a very common disease in summer, especially among children; but if attended to in time by the parents or nurses, little is required. Take good care of the little one, keep it clean, and give it healthy food; nature will take care of the rest. In case medicine is needed, we will give you a few remedies:

Aconite 3.x. in early stage. Bry. 3.x., when it appears from sudden changes in the weather. Cal. carb. 3.x., for teething children. China 6.x., great prostration. Cam. 3.x., diarrhea with colic pains. Phod. 6.x., where there is frequent changes in the color of the discharges. Baptisia 2.x., stools green and very offensive. Alternate with Gels. 3.x.

CHOLERA MORBUS.

Cholera Morbus begins with violent purging and vomiting, attended with griping in the bowels, with a constant desire to go to stool. It comes on suddenly, and is most common in autumn. There is scarce any disease more fatal and rapid than this, when proper means are not used in due time.

CAUSE.—It is occasioned by a redundancy and putrid acrimony of bile; food that easily sours on the stomach, as butter, fat pork, sweetmeats, pies and cakes, apples or melons, cherries, cucumbers, etc. It sometimes proceeds from poisonous substances taken into the stomach. It may likewise proceed from a violent passion or affection of the mind, such as fear, anger, etc.

SYMPTOMS.—It is generally preceded by heart-

burn, sour belching from the stomach and flatu-
lency, with pain in the stomach and entestines.
These are followed by excessive vomiting and purging of green, yellow and blackish-colored bile, with
distention of the stomach, and violent griping
pains. There is great thirst, and often a fixed pain
about the region of the navel. Sometimes a cold,
clammy sweat. As the disease progresses the pulse
becomes almost imperceptible, the extremities grow
cold, the urine is obstructed, there is palpitation of
the heart. Violent hiccoughing, fainting and convulsions are the signs of approaching death.

REMEDY.—Under the head of Recipes and Prescriptions you will find the author's remedy, and
how to use it.

We will also give one of the old prescriptions,
which, we have no doubt, is very good. Keep
your patient warm. Feet and extremities should
be wrapped in dry, hot blankets, hot irons and jugs
of hot water kept to the feet and limbs; mustard
draft to the stomach till the skin is quite red; and
give the following:

Ground black pepper, one tablespoonful.

Table salt, one tablespoonful.

Hot water, half tumblerful.

Cider vinegar, half tumblerful.

Mix.

Dose, one teaspoonful every few minutes till the
whole is taken.

9

It is said this may be relied upon in curing cholera morbus, and also genuine cholera.

First dose may be vomited up; if so, repeat.

Stir the medicine well each time.

HOMŒOPATHIC TREATMENT.

This disease appears suddenly, from various causes, and needs prompt attention. Use hot applications on the abdomen (dry heat the best).

After eating ice cream and rich food, Arsen. 3.x.

With colic pains, drawing one double, Coloc. 6.x.

From sudden fright, Opi. 6.x.

Vomiting of sour food or acid, Ipecac 3.x.

Diarrhea, with whitish, watery, slimy stool, without pain; quiet delirium or stupefaction, Phos. acid 6.x.

Pale face, eyes sunken, dry, yellowish coating on the tongue, great thirst, heat and burning in the abdomen, Secale, cor. 3x.

Verat. Alb. 3.x.—Pale, death-like expression of the face; tongue dry, blackish and cracked; unquenchable thirst for cold drinks, excessive vomiting of the ingesta with green mucus, also black bile; great weakness after vomiting; severe, cutting pains in the abdomen; violent diarrhea, with greenish, watery, flocculent stools, followed by rapid prostration; cramps in the calves; small, almost imperceptible pulse; hoarse, weak voice and cold breath; cold sweat over the whole body; 10 to 15 drops in half glass of water. Dose, teaspoonful every 15 to 30 minutes until relieved. The above remedies prepared and taken in the usual way.

BILIOUS OR CRAMP COLIC.

Many persons are subject to this distressing disease and suffer for hours without obtaining relief, when it is the simplest thing to cure in the world.

Take of the fluid extract of Dioscorea villosa (wild yam) 30 drops, in about one swallow of hot water, at a dose; repeat it in 30 minutes if necessary. In the meantime take one pint of warm water, add half teaspoonful of salt, stir till dissolved, and inject slowly into the bowels with a syringe. Retain it as long as possible. This will evacuate the bowels in less than 30 minutes, and you will get prompt relief.

HOMŒOPATHIC TREATMENT.

Added to the above we would prescribe hot applications externally, either dry or wet; the handiest thing is to take the stove griddle or a hot plate wrapped in a cloth and apply to the abdomen. Internally give Coloc. 6.x., 12 drops in half glass of water. Dose. teaspoonful every half hour till relieved. This remedy is strongly indicated where severe cramps exist, drawing one double.

Aloes 3.x.—Especially for elderly people, with intense griping pains accross the lower portion of the abdomen; cold perspiration and extreme prostration. Prepared and taken as above.

CRAMP IN THE PIT OF THE STOMACH.

Severe, pinching, gnawing or contractive pains in the stomach, generally occurring after taking food.

CAUSE.—Highly seasoned or indigestible food; stimulants, coffee and tobacco; long fasting, exposure to cold or damp, etc. It is usually but a symptom of indigestion.

REMEDY.—Most forms of this difficulty can be cured in a few minutes by very simple means:

Take a teacupful of hot water, add a heaping tablespoonful of sugar. Drink it slowly, and hot as possible. In some cases it may be necessary to repeat the dose in twenty or thirty minutes; but seldom more than one dose will be needed.

Another means is, place a mustard poultice on the stomach and allow it to remain till considerable redness is produced; follow this with a hot fomentation of hops or tansy. If it should occur in the night, apply friction over the stomach. Rubbing with the hand, with an active *will*, until a high degree of heat is produced; this will often afford effectual relief. However, the patient subject to these conditions should shun all articles of food which excite attacks of this kind, and live on plain, easily-digested food, spend his time in the fresh air and sunlight, and take regular active exercise.

HOMŒOPATHIC TREATMENT.

Following the above treatment to restore the health to its normal condition, use Canth. 6.x., Puls. 30.x., Arsen. 3.x., Nux Vom. 12.x.; 10 drops to usual amount of water. Dose, teaspoonful every half or one hour. Either of these remedies can be taken separately, or used in alternation if desired. For permanent relief these remedies should be continued for several days, preparing fresh each day.

FEVERS.

In fevers the nurse should understand how to manage the patient and subdue the fever before it gets to such a degree as to become threatening and dangerous. Here is where the tepid sponge-bath is practicable. Part of the body can be gone over at a time, beginning at the head; cover the body as you go. This treatment can be repeated every hour while the fever lasts, taking care that you do not sponge the patient after the fever has abated.

There is never any danger of taking cold in giving a bath during the fever.

Remember, in all cases, the head should be kept cool by bathing it with water. This can be repeated often; at the same time the feet and lower extremities should be watched closely and kept warm with hot irons, jugs of hot water, or wrapped up with hot flannels. *Follow* these rules closely and nearly every case can be controlled, and the patient made much better in a short time.

RULES TO OBSERVE.

Rule 1.—Fever patients should have nutritious food to keep up and sustain the *vital forces*. It should consist of beef extract, chicken or mutton broth, milk punch, etc., made as directed on pages 17 and 22. The food should be given at intervals, from two to three hours, little at a time. Great quantities of food are not required when sick. Never disturb or wake your patients to give them medicine or food, unless they are under the influence of narcotic medicines; for sleep will do more good than medicine. Watch them closely, and as soon as they wake be ready to give the medicine with the least disturbance, that they may become quiet and go to sleep again.

Rule 2.—See that the room is well ventilated. If it is winter, the room should be kept 60 or 70 deg. Farenheit. In summer there is not much danger of cold air, if you have clothes to regulate the temperature of the body. The lungs should have fresh air and plenty of it.

Rule 3.—Do not go from the cold air to the bed-side of the sick, especially if the patient be in a perspiration, or has rheumatism; the skin is very sensitive; you had better wait in another room till you get warm. No one has any idea of the pain and suffering of this disease unless they have had it themselves. Every joint is racked with pain, and the least touch adds to the suffering. Even the banging of a door, the shutting of a window, or the squeaking of a shoe is but adding agony to the patient, and should be avoided.

Rule 4.—Do not have old bottles sitting around. When you are through with the medicine, wash out your bottles and set them away. Medicines should never be kept for future use, for the same kind is seldom ever required again.

Rule 5—*To change the dress of patient.*— Much distress is often caused by not properly understanding how to proceed to get the arms in and out of the sleeves. If the disease is likely to continue, rip the sleeves open, then tack on some strings so they can be tied. This will not injure the garment, and it can be sewed up again when needed.

Rule 6.—There is a secret in handling a broken bone or sore limb. Never take hold with the ends of your thumb and finger, as though you were afraid of it; but take a firm grasp, or slip your hand under and let the limb lie in the palm, then support it with your thumb and finger. All nervous handling produces fear, while the firm grasp and steady nerve of the attendant quiet the patient.

SCARLET FEVER.

Children are far more liable to contract this disease than adults, as few of the latter ever have it, even when exposed. The interval between the exposure and the attack varies from two to five days to three weeks, and patients have been known to have an attack without exposure, when it is prevailing in the neighborhood.

GENERAL SYMPTOMS.—Scarlet fever usually commences very suddenly, with the usual prodroma of fever, chills and shivering, succeeded by hot skin, nausea, sometimes vomiting, with rapid pulse, thirst, frontal headache, and sore throat. The last named symptom is generally the earliest complained of by the patient. In about forty-eight hours after the occurrence of these symptoms, the characteristic rash is perceptible. first on the breast, from whence it generally extends and spreads all over the body. These eruptions are bright-red points or spots, which have been compared, by some writers, to look like a boiled lobster shell.

These spots either run together and diffuse themselves uniformly over the skin, or else appear in large, irregular patches on different parts of the body. The color of the skin disappears on pressure, but returns on its removal. The appearance of the tongue is characteristic; it is first coated, the tips and edges are red; the papillæ are red and somewhat raised; afterwards the tongue cleans off and looks very red and raw. A diffused redness, sometimes of a dark scarlet color, covers the mouth, etc., which disappears as the febrile symptoms and rash subside. About the fifth day the rash begins to decline, and entirely disappears about the eighth or ninth day, leaving the patient in a very weak condition. The process of peeling off the cuticle is varied in its duration; it takes place in the form of scurf, from the face and trunk, but from the hands and feet large flakes are separated, sometimes coming away like a glove or slipper.

This is a very dangerous disease, and should have prompt attention. We advise you to send for your physician, as it is apt to be followed by serious complications; do not attempt treatment yourself. The external treatment is the most essential, no matter what the complications are, and it is called for in every case, and your family physician, if he be an intelligent one, will not object, for it will not interfere with his internal treatment. This being a cutaneous disease, the battle-ground must be fought upon the surface; hence we should advise you by all means to give a warm sponge-bath every night, followed by greasing the entire body with an uncooked piece of bacon—in severe cases always bind thin slices of it upon the neck, breast and soles of the feet. We urge this treatment upon you, as it is called for and highly effectual. If attended to promptly it will scarce ever fail to cure the patient with but little other treatment.

HOMŒOPATHIC TREATMENT.

This disease, that rages as an epidemic among children, is dreaded, and well it may be, for it is very dangerous and should never be allowed to run long without attention. Much depends upon the care and surrounding conditions. The following remedies may be used.

Indications:—Dry, hot skin, full, frequent pulse, great restlessness, violent thirst before the eruptions make their appearance, Acon. 3.x.

Severe headache, with red face, very drowsy, muttering delirium, Bell. 3.x. Alternate with the above remedy 10 drops in half glass water. Teaspoonful every hour.

Fever of typhoid character; tongue of deep red color, nose discharging a thick, white, fetid mucus; itching and burning all over the body, Apis. 3.x.

Where the eruption is delayed or grows pale, with rapid prostration; putrid sore throat; intense thirst with internal heat and external coldness; fetid diarrhea, Arsen. 3.x.

Protracted cases, glands of the neck are swollen and hard, throat greatly inflamed.' This remedy is especially indicated in children with scrofulous diathesis. Cal. carb. 3.x.; 10 to 15 drops to half glass of water. Dose, teaspoonful every half to one and two hours, according to severity of the case.

INTERMITTENT FEVER.

This disease is commonly called fever and ague, or chills and fever, as the name implies. It is too well known by the people to need any description.

It is distinguished by the physicians under the following names: Quotidian, if the chill and fever return every day; Tertian, if it comes on every third day; Quartan, if it comes every fourth day. The length of intervals determines the variety of ague, and when these varieties duplicate, they are called double Quotidian, etc., etc.

This disease should not be allowed to run long, but should have prompt and efficient treatment at once, as it is liable to run into a chronic form and the liver, spleen and kidneys become seriously affected, and sometimes dropsy the result. We have no doubt that this disease has caused more trouble to the old-school physicians to control and cure than all other fevers combined; yet it is the most simple and easy to cure, and we will guarantee a cure every time without the use of quinine, either. Here is the prescription and treatment:

Fluid extract of Grindelia squarrosa.

Fluid extract of Eucalyptus globules, of each one ounce.

Fluid extract of Baptisia tinctora, one drachm.

Fluid extract of Podophyllum peltatum, ten drops.

Glycerine sufficient to make a six-ounce mixture. Mix.

Dose, teaspoonful every three hours, for a day or so, then three times per day until all is taken.

During this time you should take three or four alcohol sweats (see description of Turkish bath), followed each time by brisk rubbing. This treatment alone will cure this disease.

HOMŒOPATHIC TREATMENT.

Arcen. 3.x.—Chill and fever.

Bry. 3.x.—When the chill predominates.

China 3.x.—When chill is anticipated.

Eup. pur. 3.x.—With disposition to run into another chill.

Gels. 3.x.—Where fever runs high.

Ipec. 3.x.—For nausea and gastric trouble.

Nat. mur. 3.x.—Grindelia squarrosa, Berberis aquifolium, for chronic cases. Prepare and take in the usual way.

_____

PNEUMONIA.

Pneumonia is an inflammation of the lungs; it is predisposed by intense nervous depression, debility, or exhaustion. The existing cause is usually the effect of cold, damp, exposure, vicissitudes of heat and cold, inhalation of irritants, or mechanical violence. The usual mode of attack is depression of the large aerating surface of the lower lobe of the right lung. It may remain there or proceed to the left lung, then upward. In all conditions, the lungs become engorged from below upwards. Pneumonia may be met with in the following forms: acute (sudden in its character). If the patient has a strong vital force it may resist the local irritation. In others whose constitutions are more feeble, it may involve both pleura and lungs, and both be implicated at the same time. Then again, it may be complicated with typhoid.

Our book is too small to go farther in detail. Therefore, we have no room to describe pleurisy, only to say our treatment would be much the same in both diseases.

TREATMENT.—As soon as the disease is recognized, in either case, the patient should take an alcohol bath and be put to bed. The temperature of the apartment should be kept between 65 and 70 degs. Active cupping should be resorted to over the consolidated lung, followed by flaxseed poultices. The action of warmth and moisture over the affected tissues tends directly to increase its vitality, as is soon shown by diminished dyspnœa, the breath being drawn more easily. Even intercostal movement can be detected. The poultice should be made of linseed meal, because it keeps moist longer; it should be fully half an inch thick, spread on flannel sufficiently large to cover the affected part. The poultice should be changed every two hours, as the heat of the body will soon dry it. As the symptoms change for the better, change the poultice for that of compresses. Take a towel, wring it dry from tepid water, a little salt added, and apply to the chest. Change it often. Lay a dry towel over the wet one. This will prevent the underclothing from getting damp. Remember, you should keep the feet hot and moist by sponging them with water as hot as can be borne, and give the following prescription as internal treatment:

```
Fluid extract of Asclepias tuberosa
    (pleurisy root)................half drachm.
Fluid ext. Collinsonia (stone root).half drachm.
Fluid ext. Lycopus virginicus (sweet
    bugle weed)................half drachm.
Water......................three and a half ozs.
```
Mix.

Dose, teaspoonful every one or two hours.

If there is much congestion of blood to the head, give

Tincture of belladonna, 10 to 15 drops.

In half tumbler of water.

Dose, teaspoonful every hour; alternate with the above medicine, making fresh every day.

With this treatment followed you will be astonished to see how your patient will rally from this dreaded disease.

Pleurisy can be treated in the same way with success.

How different this treatment from the old way, which was done by bleeding the patient, followed by mustard drafts, and blisters all over the breast, thus adding more fuel to the already consuming inflammation and heat in the lungs. Their internal treatment was veratum, sweet spirits of nitre, calomel and jalap, carbonate of ammonium, the result of which was generally followed by a first-class funeral in the family. The attending physician was always charged with being very attentive during the sickness, and had the credit of handling the patient very skillfully.

HOMŒOPATHIC TREATMENT.

The most common cause of this disease is from cold, and if attended to in time can be easily prevented, and the patient spared a long, tedious spell of sickness and suffering.

For external treatment we recommend hot applications, either dry or wet, on the chest; soak the feet in hot water; put the patient in bed and produce free perspiration. Take the following remedies as indicated:

Acon. 3.x—In first stages.

Bry. 3.x.—Fever moderate, cough with expectoration of tenacious mucus. Alternate this with the above every hour.

Phos. 6.x.—In violent cases the stitching pains are excited or aggravated by coughing or breathing; tightness across the breast.

Verat. vir. 6.x.—When congestion and inflammation have fairly set in, high fever, with strong, quick pulse; sinking, faint feeling in pit of the stomach; constant burning distress in cardiac region; 10 drops to half glass of water. Dose, teaspoonful every half, one, or two hours, as the case demands.

CATARRH.

This is a terrible disease, which nearly if not quite three-fourths of the human family are afflicted with, more or less—from the fact few people ever dream they have anything but a slight cold or a touch of influenza, until all the mucous membranes and air passages are so affected that it has poisoned the blood and assumed a chronic form of the most distressing and loathsome disease, which seems to resist all treatment. The world has been filled with more advertisements of quack nostrums, and perhaps more money is spent in this way for the cure of catarrh than any other disease. Dear reader, let us tell you here that all the money you spend in this way is worse than useless, for you are only injured, or if benefited it is only temporary. Catarrh is an inflammation of the mucous membranes of portions of the air passages, characterized by sneezing, watery discharges from the nostrils, increased secretions from the lachrymal glands, slight headache, heavy feeling in the head, chilliness, fever, hoarseness, dry cough, sore throat. Sometimes it seems to be a drying up of all the secretions, the air passages all stopped up, with loss of appetite and feeling of lassitude.

Different names are applied to it, as it affects the schneiderian membrane—catarrhal cephalgia, when it affects the frontal sinus; bronchitis, when the stress falls upon the trachea and bronchial tubes. Catarrh, properly speaking, affects the mucous lining of the nose and throat, and is extremely prevalent and intractable. People of a strumous diathesis are most liable to this form of disease; hence, we find it of a low chronic type,

10

requiring specific treatment. If the catarrhal inflammation has been violent in scrofulistic patients,
ulceration is the result.

The peculiar influences which originate catarrh,
affect, primarily, the organic nerves which supply
the surface, and through them the system generally. Secretions and the circulation in the parts
are specially deranged; the chief modifications of
the disease from the constitutional actions are disturbed, the extent of surface involved becomes
greater and the grade of irritation proportionately
increased.

TREATMENT.—In acute attacks, an emetic of
compound powder of lobelia (as described in other
parts of this book how to prepare), followed by a
hot air bath, also foot bath. Tincture of aconite,
given as an arterial sedative, acting freely on the
secretions, from ten to fifteen drops to a third of
tumblerful of water; dose, teaspoonful every one or
two hours, as the case demands. Hot atomized
vapors to control the local inflammation. Moist
warmth is a powerful restorer in this disease, to
the arrested circulation and vital action, the safest
therapeutic agent we have, because it is direct.
The warm vapors should be allowed to come freely
in contact with the inflamed mucous membranes.
Various agents are used for inhalations with good
success. We feel partial to the sulphate of hydrastis, or golden seal, as it is called; also, the blood-

root, or the permanganate potassa. These remedies are all rapidly absorbed by the mucous membranes; the warm stream softens and relaxes the tissues. There is nothing that acts so promptly as the warm atomizers in catarrh. The atomizing instruments of the various kinds can be had at nearly all drug stores. Following we give you a table of remedies to be used and their strength.

The nasal douche is also an indispensable instrument; it washes out the air passages and keeps them cleansed and prepared to be followed by the medicine for the atomizers. For the douche, various remedies are used in alternation. To a quart of warm water (as warm as can be borne) half a teaspoonful of salt, is an excellent remedy. Chlorate of potassa, half a drachm to a quart of water, is another. The sulphate of zinc, or diluted carbolic acid, used in various strengths, are very useful. The douche, and how to use it, is too well known to take the time to describe it here.

The dose in the following table is to be added to an ounce of distilled water for the atomizing instrument. There are many remedies used in this way but we shall give only those which we have had the best success with. We give this variety of remedies because we do not know the patient to prescribe for him, leaving you to use such ones as seem to give the most relief. Then alternate them.

Sulphate of hydrastin	5 to 10	grains.
Sulphate of baptisin	10 to 20	"
Sulphate of iron	1 to 5	"
Sulphate of sanguinarin	5 to 10	"
Pulv. borax	5 to 20	"
Digitalis	½ to 1	"
Potassa chlorate	5 to 10	"
Potassa bromide	5 to 10	"
Potassa iodide	5 to 10	"
Potassa permanganate	10 to 20	"
Salt	5 to 30	"
Carbolic acid	1 to 7	"
Bichromate of Potassa	5 to 10	"

The best of the above is carbolic acid, which stimulates, deoderizes and promotes cicaterization of the abraded surfaces. During this treatment we will give you a prescription which acts as a blood purifier and is of great importance in the cure of this disease:

BLOOD PURIFIER.

Fluid extract of the Ampelopsis quing (American ivy).

Fluid extract of Menispermum (yellow parilla), of each half an ounce.

Fluid extract Dioscorea villa (wild yam root), one drachm.

Fluid extract Podophyllum, pelt (mandrake), half a drachm.

Syrup of stillingia,

Syrup of dandelion, of each equal quantity, sufficient to make a six-ounce mixture.

Mix.

Dose, teaspoonful three times a day.

This is one of the best blood purifiers in catarrh-al or scrofulistic conditions we have ever used, even in syphilitic diseases. If iodide of potassium be added two or three drachms, it is still better.

We have a catarrh snuff we consider the best ever in use. We will give that under the head of "Recipes." See Index.

HOMŒOPATHIC TREATMENT.

Bell. 3.x.—Sore throat and hoarseness, throbbing headache, worse from motion; alternate chilliness and heat.

Ipe. 3.x.—Aching pain over the eyes; fluent coryza; stoppage of the nose and loss of smell; rattling in the chest; oppressed breathing, as of asthma.

Sulph. 2.x.—Fluent coryza of clear water, sore-ness and pressure in the throat, as from a lump; complete loss of taste and smell; coldness of extrem-ities, and chilliness; frequent weak, faint spells; great liability to take cold; morning diarrhea.

Heper. sulph. 2.x.—Sore pains in dorsum, bones are sore to the touch.

Hydra. 12.x.—Thick, tenacious secretions from posterior nares, dropping down into the throat.

Kali. carb. 2.x.—Obstruction of the nose, mak-ing breathing through the nostrils impossible.

Cal. carb. 3.x.—Nose red and inflamed, discharge very offensive, severe pain in the head; adapted to persons threatened with phthisis and bronchial affections.

SPECIAL REMEDIES FOR DIFFERENT COLORED DISCHARGES.

For Green Discharge.—Kali. bich. 3.x., Natr. carb., Phosph., Puls., Rhus., Lach., Sep., Thuj.

For Yellow.—Alum, Graph., Mur. ac., Nitr. ac., Lyc.

For Thick, Whitish.—Kali. bich., Merc., Nux. vom.

For Fetid.—Aurum, Graph., Nitr. ac., Rhus.

Prepare and take these remedies in the usual way, and with close observation to hygiene much can be accomplished; medicine alone will do but little.

ASTHMA.

Asthma is a nervous disease, whose phenomena depend upon a tonic contraction of the circular muscular fibres of the bronchial tubes. Paroxysms induced by direct or reflex mechanism, that is to say, the stimulus to contraction may be central in the medulla oblongata, or it may be in the pulmonary or gastric portion of the pneumogastric, or in some other part of the nervous system. Asthma has, at the root of it, some central nervous irritation, or some peripheral source of it; it may be some latent miasma, skin disease, or some organic affection of the chest; other causes are merely exciting, as moist easterly winds, atmospheric electricity, inhalation of irritating substances, as the aroma of new mown hay, malaria, damp, variable climate, incompatibility of the individual to the location, soil, or country where he lives, etc.

SYMPTOMS.—A fit of asthma is usually preceded by headache, sleepiness, and various other causes; lassitude, pain in the head, back or limbs, loss of appetite, dry, hacking cough, depression of spirits. The attack is usually ushered in suddenly during the night, with a sensation of suffocation or constriction about the chest, urgent, distressing dyspnœa, aggravated by the slightest movement. Inspirations short and strong, while the expirations are long, labored and wheezing. Great and rapid movement of the nostrils, countenance livid and bloated, indicative of great distress and anxiety; inclined to retain the erect posture, with an intense struggle for breath. On auscultation no respiratory murmur is audible, but vibrating murmur loud and wheezing, or shrill whistling; pulse small and feeble, eyes staring, anxious countenance; temperature of surface falls to 82 deg. Fahr.; but after a while the fatigue causes the skin to pour out abundant perspiration, and after a period comes

relief; cough with expectoration of ropy, stringy
mucus.   Paroxysm ceases and the patient falls
asleep.   During the intervals of attacks the patient
usually enjoys good health.   It is frightful to anyone who never witnessed a person with a spasm of
asthma; it is not a dangerous disease, by any
means, but a most distressing one.

There have been many remedies introduced
which have, in many cases, afforded temporary
relief, such as common brown paper soaked in a
solution of saltpetre, then dried, after which burn
it in a tight room, that the patient may inhale the
smoke.   Also, drying the leaves of the Jamestown
weed and smoking them in a pipe or paper. These
only bring temporary relief.

TREATMENT.—When the spasm is on give the
patient a teaspoonful of the compound tincture of
lobelia every five minutes until relieved, followed
with a half drachm dose of bromide potassium.   This will seldom fail to relieve the bronchial spasm; but the final cure of asthma lies in
the constitutional treatment in the intervals of the
attack, by the use of a nutritious diet, the alcohol
vapor bath three or four times a week, followed by
brisk friction with the hands, and regular hygienic
habits; food easily digested; the dyspeptic condition of the stomach must be relieved, and all the internal organs put in good condition; the hot air
bath (see description of bath) will do it if properly

administered. The cause in all cases should be ascertained and the patient placed in a location compatible with his idiosyncrasies and close attention paid to the general health.

Excellent results will be followed by using the following prescription:

> Fluid extract Grindelia robusta (new
> remedy)......... .... half ounce.
> Fluid extract Silphum (rosinweed).. half ounce.
> Tincture of Lobelia seed............ half drachm.
> Bromide potassa...... .... half ounce.
> Hydrocyanic acid, diluted........... 25 drops.
> Extract of malt.................... three and half ozs.
> Distilled water sufficient to make a six-ounce mixture.

Mix.

Dose, one teaspoonful one hour after each meal, and one on going to bed, continued for one week or more.

This prescription, with the constitutional treatment, will effectually cure this disease.

HOMŒOPATHIC TREATMENT.

The constitutional and hygienic mode of treatment of the above we fully agree with, but to accomplish a permanent cure for this distressing disease, we have only to add a few of our best remedies with their special indications.

Cal. carb. 3.x.—For chronic asthma, with tight breathing and tension in the chest, as if from rush of blood, relieved by raising the shoulders; desire to take deep breath, and sensations as if the breath remained stopped between the scapulæ; the patient loses his breath by merely stooping; patient suffering with dry cough, especially toward morning; 15 drops in half glass of water. Dose, teaspoonful every hour.

Grindelia Robusta, 3.x.—Purely nervous asthma where inhalation is easy, expectoration difficult; fear of going to sleep on account of loss of breath, which awakens him. Cardiac asthma, cough from reflex causes; chronic bronchitis; 15 to 20 drops in half glass of water. Dose, every 30 minutes until relieved, then prolong the intervals.

Ipe. 3.x.—Difficult expiration; violent constriction of throat and chest; peculiar panting sound; gasps for air at the open window; face pale, worse from least motion; threatened suffocation, with nightly suffocative fits; constant cough raising nothing, although chest seems full of phlegm; cough sometimes followed by vomiting, which relieves; 12 drops in half glass of water; teaspoonful every 30 minutes till better.

Tartar emetic, 2.x.—Especially suitable to old people; difficult breathing, and shortness of breath, with desire to sit erect; oppression and suffocative fits, coming on suddenly, especially in the evening or in the morning; mucus and rattling in chest; suffocative cough, with violent palpitation of the neart; gasping for breath; 10 to 15 drops in half glass of water.—Teaspoonful every 15 to 30 minutes until relieved, then prolong the intervals.

Kali. phos. 3.x.—Nervous asthma, with depression after the most immoderate use of food; sallow features, sunken eyes, emaciation; 10 drops to half glass of water. Teaspoonful every hour.

The best results, from our latest experience we have found in the two following remedies, given in the usual way:

Symphytum and Myosotis. 3.x.—They seem to have the widest range of cure and cover more indications than any others.

NEURALGIA.

This is a terrible disease which some of the human family are afflicted with. Therefore, it is very important for those who suffer from it to be prepared with a few remedies, and with their judicious use it is not necessary for one to suffer long.

REMEDY 1.—Take half a teaspoonful of sal-ammoniac, and four tablespoonfuls of camphor-water; mix. Dose, teaspoonful every ten minutes, until relieved; if necessary, increase the dose.

Camphor-water may be prepared by adding one teaspoonful of strong spirits of camphor to half teacupful of water.

One remedy will scarcely ever cure all cases of this disease. It is useless to treat it with liniments; fomentations are much better. The sweat bath repeated several times is the most reliable permanent cure we know of (see discription of bath). In case you have not these facilities the following treatment may be resorted to: First. Soak the feet 30 minutes in hot water, adding a tablespoonful of ground mustard, at the same time drinking hot ginger tea, or, better still, a tea made from smart weed (this is excellent). Go to bed; add a few bottles of hot water to the feet and limbs; cover with sufficient clothing to produce free perspiration, keeping it up from 30 to 40 minutes. While you are sweating you should rub and scratch your body thoroughly, in order to remove the morbid accumulation, which is so abundantly secreted in the pores of the skin. Then sponge the body with tepid water; dry with a towel; then rub briskly with the hands for a few moments. With this treatment we have never failed to cure the most persistent cases.

HOMŒOPATHIC TREATMENT.

With the above external treatment we will add a few remedies, to be taken internally:

GELS. 3.x. Special Indications: Throbbing pain in back part of the head, extending through to the forehead and eyes; heaviness of eye-lids, and con-fusion of mind. 10 drops added to half glass of water. Dose, teaspoonful every half to one hour, according to severity of case.

Acon. 3.x.—Red and hot face; severe pain on one side; great fear and anxiety; pains worse at night, with great restlessness; prepare as above.

Bryonia 6.x.—Pressing, tearing, shooting pains; worse from motion, feels better when lying on the affected side, rheumatic disposition and great irri-tability. Prepare as above. Dose, teaspoonful every one to two hours.

Sulphite of nickle. 3.x.—This is a new remedy, lately introduced to the profession by Prof. Hale, of Chicago, in which he claims for it a *specific* for periodical neuralgia. Prepare and take in usual way.

SICK HEADACHE.

This distressing disease has received its name from the constant nausea, or sickness of the stom-ach, which attends the pain in the head.

Symptoms.—The pain is apt to begin in the morning, on waking from a deep sleep, or after sleeping in a closed room, or when some irregular-ity of diet has been indulged in several days pre-vious. There is an oppressive feeling in the head, which gradually increases into a severe pain in the

temples or top of the head, followed by a deathly
sickness at the stomach, with a sense of tenderness
on pressure, and sometimes vomiting.

REMEDY.—The quickest way to relieve this distressing sickness is to empty the stomach at once
by an emetic, which can be produced by drinking
slowly a large quantity of blood-warm water, with
enough salt to be tasted. This will wash and
cleanse the stomach of all its morbid contents. At
the same time you should place your feet in hot
water; this will induce perspiration, which is highly
necessary. As soon as the stomach becomes a little
quiet you can commence drinking lemon water,
prepared in the following manner:

Two gills of tepid water, add one teaspoonful of
oil or the clear juice of lemon; drink every fifteen
minutes for one hour. Persons of strong constitutional habits may add more to each dose. We have
cured hundreds of cases in this simple manner.
Often in three hours the patient would be as well
as ever, and could go about his work as well as
usual.

More than one-fourth of the female portion have
experienced sick headache, in a greater or less degree, ever since salaratus was introduced and used
as an ingredient in making bread and pastries; and
the sooner it is dispensed with the less of this affection there will be.

When there is acidity of the stomach two teaspoonfuls of pulverized willow charcoal dissolved in half teacupful of soda water (baking soda), taken at one dose, will cure this form. There are many other kinds of headache, arising from other causes too numerous to mention. Some are from loss of nerve, or vital force, and some are produced by excess of mental labor or deep sorrow. These forms are readily cured by the magnetic power of another person, commonly called Human Magnetism, with which most persons are perfectly familiar.

Human Magnetism is a potent agent in the cure of all diseases to which the human body is heir to, when properly used. Many physicians are curing disease in this way, at the present day, without the use of any medicine, and many of them very successful. The author will give you an essay on the Philosophy of Human Magnetism in the closing chapter of this book.

HOMŒOPATHIC TREATMENT.

Little need be said on this subject. The best and only way to get rid of it is to take care of the general health, close attention to diet, plenty of out-door exercise, etc.

It is not a disease, only a symptom, caused by some derangement of the system. Usually affects those of a bilious temperament. For temporary relief and to assist nature, we will give the following remedies:

Great tenderness of epigastric region to pressure; burning heat in stomach; sharp shooting pains; vomiting of all food and drink.   Arsen. 3.x.

Congestion of blood to head, with throbbing headache; delirium, with desire to escape from bed; photophobia (or dread of light).   Bell. 3.x.

When vomiting and nausea are the most prominent features; bitter green mucus, with slight diarrhea.   Ipe. 3.x.

Face red and bloated; tongue red, clean and tremulous; vomiting of sour mucus; constipation with hard, difficult stool; always worse in the morning.   Nut. vom. 3.x.

Great tenderness in region of stomach; intense thirst for cold drink, but inability to retain anything on the stomach; cold extremities; covered with cold perspiration; extreme prostration, with anguish and fear of death.   Verat. alb. 3.x.   Prepare and give in the usual way.   Alternate any two remedies, if desired.

DYSPEPSIA.

Dyspepsia is more than a disease of the stomach, and means more than indigestion.   The monster of civilization.   It is a disease of both sexes, all ages, and all conditions. Infants are born with it, aged people die with it. Its symptoms are legion. Among them are a morbid appetite, acid eructations, heartburn, painful fullness, distention, or weight of the stomach, nausea, vomiting, emaciation, colic, constipation, diarrhea, general debility, depression of spirits, vertigo, headache, dimness of vision, sleeplessness, palpitation of the heart, slow pulse, coated tongue, fetid breath, dullness of all the senses, insanity, suicide, etc., etc. The seat of the disease is in the central ganglia of the organic system of nerves, which preside over the secretion of the gastric juice, and genarally over the digestive and assimulative processes.

The causes, effects, and relations of dyspepsia cover almost the whole ground of pathology; and as we have already said, is hereditary. It may come from either parent; we have no occasion to doubt this, for children take after their parents in much less important particulars. The diet of the nurse may give an infant dyspepsia. Whatever will give the mother or nurse this disease, will so affect the milk as to cause it in the child. Eating too much food will cause dyspepsia; eating too fast, preventing mastication and insalivation; eating hot food and hot drinks enfeeble the stomach; indigestible food, as new bread, short cakes, pastry, sweetmeats, pickles, and greasy meats, and all that sort of thing. We exhaust the power of

11

an organ if we overtask it, and cause disease. All spirituous and narcotic beverages, tea, coffee, and alcoholic drinks, and above all, *tobacco*—by its direct action upon the nervous system, by its acrid, irritating character, and the constant excitement of the salivary glands and waste of this secretion by the excessive spitting of the smoker and chewer. Any kind of exhaustion, either mentally or physically, eating a hearty meal, then take violent exercise, or get excited by joy or grief, and digestion is suspended. When the process of digestion begins, the vital power gathers around the digestive organs. The blood goes to the stomach. Now, if this be drawn off or divided, the work is badly done, the blood is poor and half vitalized; poor blood makes poor gastric juice, poor gastric juice makes poor blood, and so it goes on in a progression of badness. Added to all these causes, is exhaustion from amativeness, solitary or social; and you are near the root of evil. This list might be prolonged to an indefinite extent, but space forbids, and we proceed to give the treatment.

TREATMENT.—Diet is of the greatest importance; in every form of this disease it should be regulated by the most nutritious and easily digested food, such as milk, soups, beef tea, buttermilk, very soft-boiled eggs, grains of all kinds, and good, ripe fruit. Both food and drink should be taken in small quantities. Active exercise in the open air, with cheerful mental occupation inculcated, with perfect regularity of habits. In the majority of cases the cutaneous system is more or less involved, and it is highly essential that it should be attended to by the hot air bath, followed by the most vigorous rubbing of the body. (See description of bath). The following prescription for internal treatment will greatly assist in a permanent cure:

Fluid extract of columbo root.........half ounce.
Fluid extract of tag-elder............half ounce.
Diluted Phosphoric acid.............three drachms.
Syrup of wild cherry.................
Syrup of lemon, of each sufficient to
  make a six-ounce mixture.

Mix.
Dose, teaspoonful after each meal, and one on going to bed.

HOMŒOPATHIC TREATMENT.

The above external treatment is very necessary, and should be followed with great perseverance; much depends upon the condition the surface of the body is in. If the hot air bath is not obtainable, the sponge bath will act as a substitute; use tepid water, add a little salt; dry and rub briskly with the hands; in connection with this treatment we will give a few special remedies for internal use:

Ammon. mur. 3.x.—Lymphatic subjects, without energy; all mucous secretion increased and retained; little eructations, thirst for acids, regurgitation of food, hawking up of sour mucus; nausea after each meal, heat and fullness of the stomach; bloatedness of the abdomen, distress immediately after each meal.

Allium. sat. 3.x.—Long standing dyspepsia, especially in old, fleshy people whose bowels are disturbed by the slightest deviation from the regular diet; copious flow of saliva after eating; belching or heartburn after every change of diet.

Arsen. 3.x.—Dyspepsia, with heartburn and gulping up of acid, burning fluid, which seems to excoriate the throat; red and irritated tongue, which feels heated and rough; burning heat in the stomach and abdomen; nausea and vomiting, especially after drinking cold water; desire for food, and still does not feel like eating when set before them; sudden weakness, cold extremities.

Baptisia. 3.x.—Great sinking of the epigastrium, with frequent fainting; irritation of stomach, showing itself by violent pains over the whole cardiac region; tongue brown in the center and red at the edges; nausea with want of appetite, and constant desire for water; general debility, trembling, weak, soft pulse.

Puls. 3.x.—Slow digestion, tongue lined with a tenacious, white mucus, slimy and bitter taste, feeling of tightness after each meal, so that the

clothes must be removed or loosened; sense of pressure at the pit of the stomach, pain immediately
after eating. Alternate this remedy with Cal.
carb., 3.x.; 10 drops to half glass water. Dose, teaspoonful every hour.

For pregnant females, Acon., Arsen., Ferr., Ipec.,
Lach., Phos., Puls., Sep.

For old people, Baryt. carb., Carb. veg., China.,
Nux vom.

For sexual abuse, Cal. carb., Merc. cor., Nux
vom., Phos. acid.

Staph.—For over-loading or deranging the stom-
ach, Arsen., Ipec., Nux vom., Puls., Carb. veg.,
Lach., Sulph., Bell., China, Merc. cor., Natr. carb.,
Rhus. Prepare and administer in the usual way.
They can be alternated if desired.

SORE EYES.

Chronic or acute sore eyes may be cured easily
and in the most simple way: Melt a piece of ice,
put in a vessel, and keep for future use; to a teacupful of this add two or three grains of salt; it
should be used warm; bathe the eyes three or four
times a day; be sure the hands are clean before
bathing, to avoid any irritating substance getting
in the eye; if there be much inflammation, use a
poultice made from the raw potato scraped very

fine, apply on going to bed; a compress of cold
water is excellent, and many times all that is necessary; close attention should be paid to the general
health; never use the same towel the second time,
nor allow others to use it, as the disease is many
times transmitted in this way. If only one eye be
affected, great care should be taken in every way
not to inoculate the other by using the same towels,
or handling without washing the hands after treating the sore eye. Too much light is not beneficial,
but plenty of fresh air is all important; they should
always be protected from the wind and dust. A
few of our constitutional remedies are all that will
be required to restore them to their normal condition. Cal. carb., Hep., sulph., Graph., Sil., Puls.,
Arsen., Merc. cor., taken in the usual way, only
prolong the time between the doses.

PARALYSIS.

This disease consists of a partial or total loss of
voluntary motion or sensation; in some cases both
are destroyed. It usually occurs without coma, or
loss of consciousness or derangement of the intellectual powers, unless it be merely a derangement
of memory. It may be called general when it affects the whole body; sometimes it is followed by
apoplexy. It usually appears suddenly, without

warning by previous symptoms. Generally one side of the body is attacked, and the patient loses power of motion and sensation; then, again, only one arm or one leg is affected, and it may extend to other parts of the body.

CAUSE.—Brain affection, inflammation or effusion, abscess, softening, or blood poisoning, by opium or tobacco; disease of the kidneys, chorea, also disease of the spinal chord, excessive sexual appetite, masturbation, etc.

TREATMENT.—If the patient be young and vigorous, an active course of treatment should be pursued to diminish the pressure on the brain. Mustard applied from the extremities to the knees, with strict attention to diet and hygiene, bathing and frictionizing the body with the hands; this is a stubborn disease to deal with, and magnetism is the most potent remedy we know of. It will yield to magnetic treatment from the loving hand of a friend, when all else fails. You must have confidense and patience with this disease, and treatment for it is slow to yield.

Electricity is also good, but it must be applied by one who thoroughly understands the application.

The following prescription we have found the best:

Oil of olive, one ounce.
Oil of cinnamon,
Oil of cloves, of each one drachm.

Muriate of ammonia, two and a half drachms.
Aqua opium,
Alcohol, of each two ounces.
Water, sufficient to make a four-ounce mixture.
Mix well.

Apply this lotion to the affected parts twice a day with the hand. Rub well.

HOMŒOPATHIC TREATMENT.

We consider the use of electricity and manipulating invaluable in the cure of this disease; and, in addition, will add a few remedies to assist, to be taken internally:

Alumina. 2.x.—Paralysis from spinal disease; rheumatic and traumatic paralysis in gouty patients; arms feel heavy, as if gone to sleep; great heaviness in lower limbs, can scarcely drag them when walking, he staggers, and must sit down; numbness of head when stepping, pain in the soles of the foot when stepping, as though it were too soft and swollen; great exhaustion of strength, especially after walking in the open air, accompanied by yawning, stretching, drowsiness, wants to lie down, mistakes in speaking, consciousness of his own identity, but gets confused.

Anacardium. 3.x.—Paralysis of single parts. Sensation of weakness in arms, with trembling numbness of the fingers, wave-like twitches here and there in the legs, loss of will, cannot contract the voluntary muscles, cannot speak, only utters unintelligible words, drinks run out of the mouth, pulse slow, body cold.

Angusturæ. 3.x.—Weakness of the whole body, as if the marrow of the bones were stiff, affections of spinal cord and extensor muscles, twitching and jerking along the back like electric shocks, etc., etc.

Apis. mel. 3.x.—Spinal affection, perfectly powerless; cannot take hold of anything, has to be fed and nursed; shortening of tendons, especially lower limbs; amaciated, and cold to the touch, œdema of the feet and limbs, effusion of joints, twitching on one side of the body, while the other is paralyzed; twitching of eyeballs, with general feeling of lassitude and depression.

Arsenicum. 3.x.—Especially of the lower limbs; trembling of limbs (in drunkards); sensation of weakness, as if bruised in the small of the back, stiffness in spinal column, beginning in region of os. coccygis.

Baryta carb. 3.x.—Paralysis from apoplexy of old people, who are childish; sensorium not clear, loss of speech, trembling of hands and limbs, great weariness, constant inclination to lie down, failure of memory.

Bryonia. 6.x.—Paralysis of limbs, rheumatic and gouty pains in limbs, worse from motion and contact, legs so weak they will scarcely hold him, tot-

ter and knock together when walking. 10 drops
to half glass of water. Dose, teaspoonful every
half, one or two hours, as the case demands. As
the patient improves prolong the intervals. Par-
alysis of the tongue and organs of speech.—First.
Arn., Baryt., Bell., Caust., Cocc., Dulc., Hep., sulph..
Lach. Second. Acon., Gels., Hydrast., Stram. Of
the fingers.—First. Calc., Sec., Sil. Second. Puls.,
Amb., Cupr. Of the feet and arms.—Arn., Chin.,
Oleand., Plumb., Cina., Bry., Dulc., Gels. Of the
Bladder.—Bell., Ars., Canth., Hyos., Lach., Lyc.,
Gels., Ergot., Poisoning by Lead.—Cupr. met.,
Opium, Plat. Prepare and give in the usual way,
every half, one or two hours, as case may require.

EPILEPSY.

This is a chronic disease, and consists of periodical convulsions, unconsciousness and loss of feeling
during the attack. This dreadful disease is more
common than one would suppose, as statistics
prove that one out of every thousand is subject to it.

CAUSES.--Hereditary transmission, intemperance,
venereal excesses, self-abuse, blows on the head,
fright, and the effects of heat during hot weather.

SYMPTOMS.—Warning of the attack occurs, in a
minority of cases, by headache, dizziness, terror,
spectral allusions, or the epileptic aura. This is a

sensation like a current of air, and begins either in a hand or foot, or in the spine, proceeding towards the brain. In a large majority of cases the attack commences with a violent scream, the patient falls down unconscious and convulsions occur. Foaming at the mouth, grinding of the teeth, and biting is common; the face becomes bluish-purple, and there are erratic, involuntary muscular movements. Breathing is generally labored. The duration of the fit is from five to ten minutes. The interval between the attacks may be from a few hours to several months.

TREATMENT.—During the intervals the general health should be improved with good diet, exercise in the open air, daily bathing, occasionally vapor bath, etc.; and, above all, we should endeavor to suspend the explosion of the nervous system with large doses of bromide of potassium in doses from ten grains to a drachm two or three times daily, and continue until we are able to effect a cure by other means. We have had great success in curing many cases with the bromide of calcium, the bromide of ammonium, and bromide of lithium, in from one grain doses up to twenty grains, three or four times a day. Sometimes we use one, sometimes the other. The bromide of calcium is an excellent remedy in convulsions of little children during dentition and diarrhea or vomiting. It takes the place of all other sedatives in doses from one to twenty grains. One grain for every year up to twenty, is the standard dose.

In this disease we have had some happy results from the following prescription:

Camphor water, four ounces.

Bromide of potassium, one ounce.

Bromide of ammonia, one-half ounce.

Potass. bicarbonate, two drachms.

Tincture of calabar bean, one-half drachm.

Tincture of belladonna, thirty drops.

Mix.

Dose, teaspoonful every three hours.

If the disease is clearly connected with other causes, which only give rise to reflex irritation, of syphilitic, mercurial, or any other morbid condition of the blood, our treatment is always attended with decided success. But if the disease depends upon exostosis on the interior of the skull, or upon some organic disease, we can do but little—only mitigate its severity.

HOMŒOPATHIC TREATMENT.

To the above external treatment we will add a few remedies that will greatly assist:

Cuprum. 3.x.—Nocturnal epilepsy, or when the fit returns at regular intervals, (menses) beginning with a sudden scream; unconsciousness, loss of sensibility and throwing the body upwards and forwards, convulsion commencing at the fingers or toes, or in the arms, with coldness of the hands and feet; palor and lividity of the face, clenching the thumbs, suffocative paroxysms, frequent emission of urine; often a sign of feeble muscular action of the heart, coldness of hands and feet, etc , etc.

Camphora. 2.x.—Fits, with stertorous breathing, red and bloated face, coma. Early enough given it may prevent the fit, or at least, abridge its intensity and duration.

Glonoin. 2.x.—Fits accumulate and return daily, convulsions from cerebral congestion; stupidity and somnolence; alternate congestion of heart and head; violent, throbbing pains in the epigastrium.

Kali. brom. 2.x.—Mental hebetude, slowness of expression, failure of memory, confusion, great heat in the head, vertigo, dull, stupid expression. The whole body gives up to lassitude.

Stramonium. 3.x.—Epileptiform spasm; thrusting the head continually in quick succession to the right, continual rotary motions with the left arm; pain in pit of the stomach, obstinate constipation, deep, snoring sleep; *risus sardonicus*; pale, worn-out appearance, with a stupid, friendly look; afraid to be left alone; convulsions affecting the upper more than the lower extremities.

Lachesis 3.x.—Characterized by cries, falling down unconsciously, foam at the mouth, sudden and forcible protusion of the tongue, vertigo, heavy and painful head, palpitation of the heart, etc.

Nux. vom. 6.x.—Spinal epilepsy, with trembling or convulsive twitching of the limbs; involuntary defectation of urination, rigidity of the limbs, pressure on solar plexus renews the attack.

Silicea. 2.x.——Nocturnal epilepsy, especially about the time of the new moon, chronic cases, before the attack; feeling of great coldness of the left side of the body, shaking of the left arm; slumber with sudden starting; the spasm spreads suddenly, undulating from solar plexus up to the brain; violent screaming, groaning, tears drop out of his eyes, foam before the mouth, afterwards warm perspiration, etc., etc. Alternate this remedy with Calc. carb. 10 drops of each to half glass of water. Dose, teaspoonful every one or two hours.

CATALEPSY.

This remarkable disease of the brain and nervous system is characterized by a sudden deprivation of senses, intelligence and voluntary motion, the patient retaining the same position during the paroxysm as that held at the moment of the attack, or in which he may be placed during its continuance. Seizure may last a few minutes, several hours or days; attack intermittant, without regard to regularities of periods, there may be premonitory symptoms, as headache, mutability of temper, yawning, vertigo, palpitation, slight spasm of mind, confusion of senses; but generally appears suddenly. The eyes are fixed, either open or shut, pupils dilated. Restoration or recovery occurs suddenly, accompanied with sighing, pain or confusion in the head, with no recollection of what has transpired. No efforts to restore consciousness are effectual. Nervous and hysterical women are most liable to be affected. Catalepsy differs from ecstacy, somnambulism or clairvoyance in its being associated with a diseased condition; the other states being produced by voluntary effort. Absence of mind— a mild form of catalepsy; mesmerism and spiritualism also a species. There is little danger in a large majority of cases. It may, however, end in apoplexy, insanity or softening. It is often associated with some organic affection of the brain. Pre-disposing causes may be anything that diminishes vital power, and increases the susceptibility of the nervous system—depressing passions, hereditary debility, intense mental debility or labor, nervous exhaustion. Exciting causes are violent mental applications, mental emotions, fright, terror, suppression of menses, ovarian troubles, etc., etc.

TREATMENT.—This must be alterative, tonic and hygienic, and be directed by the general principles which govern us in the forms of disease with which it is connected. Usually, we have derived the most satisfactory results from alternating hot and cold water poured on the nape of the neck from a height. Internally give phosphorus, quinine and iron, alternated with three drops of calabar bean every two hours.

HOMŒOPATHIC TREATMENT.

It is unnecessary to speak farther on this subject, as the above covers all the ground. We can only impress upon you the necessity of adhering strictly to its teachings, and add remedies that are especially called for to aid in restoring the general health.

If caused by anger or vexation, Cham., Bry. If caused by fright, Acon., Bell., Ign., Opii. If by sudden joy, Coffea. If by grief, Ign., Phosph. Acid., Staph. If by jealousy, Hyosc., Lach. If by sexual erethism. Can., Plat., Stram. If by disappointed love, Ign., Hyocs., Lach. If by religious excitement, Stram., Sulp., Veratr. alb., China., Nux. vom. Use the 3.x. Prepare and take in the usual way.

ST. VITUS' DANCE (CHOREA).

This singular disease is recognized by want of control of the muscular nerves over the motor, in the waking state, which gives rise to irregular, tremulous and ludicrous movements of the voluntary muscles. It occurs most in girls of feeble constitutions, of irritable, nervous temperament, between the ages of six and fifteen. It is rarely met with in boys.

CAUSE.—It is from want of harmony between the gray and white matter of the cord, or it may occur from anemia, dyspepsia, skin eruptions, retarded catamenia, constipation, cold, insufficient food, excessive loss of blood, pregnancy, disease of the bladder, uterus, or mental emotion, etc.

TREATMENT.—This, of all other diseases, has baffled the skill of more physicians than any other, and yet it is more easy and simple to cure, because we have, in nearly all cases, found congestion of the entire capillary system. Hence, we have directed our treatment almost entirely to the surface; first sponging the body with tepid water, followed by anointing thoroughly with goose grease or a liniment lotion, which we intend to give under the head of Recipes and Prescriptions. After several days of this treatment give alcohol sweat baths two or three times a week, with brisk rubbing of the entire body; magnetism is the all-important remedy in this disease. The bowels must be kept open, and strict attention paid to diet; good, nutritious food is very necessary.

HOMŒOPATHIC TREATMENT.

This annoying disease, affecting a portion of the human family, is very tedious, but not difficult to cure, with proper treatment. A patient suffering from this should have pleasant surroundings, the mind should be kept occupied, so as to divert it from their own condition; plenty of fresh air and sunlight, with the above treatment closely followed, will restore the patient to their normal condition. To assist and make the cure more rapid we will add a few remedies:

Agricus. 3.x.—Chronic spasms when awake, quiet when asleep; spasmodic motion, from simple, involuntary motions and jerks of single muscles to dancing of the whole body; frequent nictitation of eyelids, redness of eyes, sensitiveness of the lumbar vertebræ, body convulsed, as if a galvanic battery were applied to the spine, worse during a thunder storm; itching spots on the skin, idiotic expression of face, inarticulate speech, ravenous appetite, but difficult deglutition; cervical glands swollen, spinal column very sensitive to pressure or to hot sponge, weakness and coldness of limbs, skin very rough.

Cim. 3.x.—From rheumatic and other causes.

Cupr. 3.x.—Periodical chorea, muscular contortions, with laughter, grimaces, exaltations, ecstacies, irregular movements, commencing in fingers and toes; better when lying down.

Scutellaria. 3.x.—Hysteric chorea, nightly rest-lessness, with frightful dreams.

Cina. 3.x.—Movements often commence with a shriek; the tongue, larynx, esophagus affected, causing a clucking from the throat to the stomach, like water poured from a bottle; staring eyes.

Crocus. 3.x.—Spasmodic contraction of a single set of muscles; jumping, dancing, laughing, whist-ling, wants to kiss everybody, epstaxis (or nose bleed) of dark stringy blood; changeable disposition, from joy to grief.

Sepia. 3.x.—Uterine chorea, associated with men-strual irregularities; eruptions like ring-worms around the body; better after the menses are over. 10 or 15 drops in half glass of water. Teaspoon-ful every hour.

Chorea caused by dysmenorrhea, amenorrhea, Puls 3.x. and Cal. carb., alternate.

Spinal Chorea, after the use of allopathic reme-dies, with crawling sensation in the parts attacked, constipation. Nux. vom., Cocc., China., Chell.

Facial Chorea, arms and legs in constant motion, unable to undress without assistance, frontal head-ache, grating of the teeth. Mygale., Bell., Hyos., China., Nux vom., Sulph. Prepare and give as usual.

CHRONIC RHEUMATISM.

This sometimes follows the acute form, and at other times it is a separate constitutional affection, coming on quite independent of any previous attack. This disease is generally very obstinate, prone to recur, and often worse at night. In time, the affected limbs lose their power of motion, from the membranes and joints being affected, the muscles sometimes become permanently contracted, and lameness the result. Usually there is but little fever, no perspiration and less swelling than in acute. This form is often the result of uncured acute rheumatism. It may be limited to one part of the body, or extend to several, and it may be fixed or shifting. The author's extended experience has led us to believe that rheumatism is a disease of the blood. Hence, to expect a cure by the use of liniments, as is usually supposed, is perfectly absurd. However, we often prescribe them for temporary relief, until we have time for the action of other curative remedies. The cause of rheumatism in different individuals is varied. In some persons it is from an alkaline condition of the fluids of the body, but in most individuals it is from an acrid condition.

Hence, the treatment should be varied. In some we give the bicarbonate of soda, 10 grains at a dose, repeated two or three times a day. In others, we give the diluted muriatic acid, half an ounce to five ounces of water; teaspoonful in a tumblerful of water, and use it as a drink.

At the same time you can take the following prescription:

Fluid extract of Cimicifuga racemosa
    (black cohosh)..................... 1 drachm.
Fluid ext. Phytolacca decandra (poke
    root)............................ 1 drachm.
Fluid extract of Colchicum........... 1 drachm.
Syrup of ginger..................... 4 ounces.

Mix.

Dose, teaspoonful every three hours.

Use the following liniment for external use:

Oil of cedar........................ 1 ounce.
Oil of sassafras.................... 1 ounce.
Oil of amber........................ 1 ounce.
Oil of olive........................ 1 ounce.
Hartshorn .. .. 1 ounce.
Spirits of camphor.................. 1 ounce.
Spirits of turpentine............... 1 ounce.
Tincture of laudanum .... 1 ounce.
Tincture of capsicum................ 1 ounce.
Alcohol............................. 1 pint.

Mix.

Apply twice a day, and keep the parts well wrapped with flannel.

This treatment, persisted in, with the alcoholic sweat bath (see description of bath), taken two or three times a week, will cure any ordinary case.

The following is a new remedy that is highly recommended and published as an effectual cure:

" Take the common garden celery, cut it into small pieces and boil in water until soft. Of this liquor let the patient drink freely three or four times a day. To use it as an article of diet prepare it in the following way: Take new milk, with a little flour added; put into a sauce-pan a little nutmeg, and simmer gently, serve it warm with toast, and this painful ailment will soon yield."

Such is the declaration of an eminent physician, who has tried it again and again with uniform success.

After this painful disease is broken up the following prescription should be used, as it acts promptly on the kidneys, carrying the disease out of the system. It is also good in any kidney troubles:

> Fluid extract of Eupatorium purpu-
> 　reum (Queen of the Meadow).... one and a half ozs.
> Fluid extract of Asclepias tuberosa
> 　(pleurisy root).................... 1 drachm.
> Fluid extract of Sanguinaria cana-
> 　densis (blood root)............... 10 drops.
> Nitrate potass....................... 3 drachms.
> Glycerine sufficient to make a 4-ounce mixture.

Mix.

Dose, teaspoonful every three hours.

HOMŒOPATHIC TREATMENT.

This disease is divided in two forms, chronic and acute. It arises from many causes. The safest and surest way is to begin treatment at its first appearance, and, if possible, avoid the dreaded affliction. In chronic the results are usually serious, and complicated with other diseases. The system should be kept in a healthy condition and close attention paid to hygiene, assisted with remedies, as indicated in the case. For acute cases we apply externally to the parts affected cotton batten, thoroughly sprinkled with powdered sulphur; bind closely on to exclude the air; keep the patient warm with an even temperature; rub the parts gently when the bandages are changed, once or twice a day; give internally Acon. 3.x.—Salicylie acid., Arsen., Asclep., Caul.; if the tongue be white and slimy, begin with Salicylate of Soda.

Chronic Rheumatism.—With swelling of joints, Acon., Anti., Apis. Apoc. cann., Asclep. tub., China., Calch., Rhus., Ham., Lyc., Nux. vom.

Erratic (or wandering pains).—First. Bry., Nux. mosch., Nux. vom., Puls. Second. Arn., Arsen., Bell., Plumbum. Sabin., Sep., Sulph. Alternate these if desired.

Rheumatism affected by every change of weather. —Bry., Cal. carb., Carb. veg., Dulc., Graph., Lach., Merc., Sil., Sulph. Prepare in the usual way; take the same, only in severe cases, then take every 30 minutes.

SPERMATORRHEA.

(MASTURBATION, OR SELF-ABUSE.)

Under this title it will be necessary to consider Masturbation (or Self-Abuse), Seminal Weakness, Sexual Exhaustion, Sterility, etc.

Masturbation is a name given to a pernicious and destructive habit—a discharge of the seminal fluids by the stimulus of the virile organs with the hand—an act which is revolting to humanity and destructive to every feeling and faculty of vigorous manhood. The great and good in all ages and nations of the world, as well as the highest medical authority condemn this pernicious, baneful practice, as fatal to the vitality of the person, entailing on himself a lower type of manhood, and even transmitting to his posterity a structure so degrading that its very constituents are disease, weakness and death. In a very large percentage of nocturnal emissions and enlarged prostate glands, masturbation has been the cause. Nationally speaking, it exercises a disastrous effect, producing imbecility, cerebral disease of every form, placing the person lower in the scale of being. But aside from all this general type of degeneration, it creates certain local diseases, such as inflammation of the prostrate glands. This is produced by an unnatural act, being an irritant by the retention of semen in the ejaculatory ducts, producing inflammation. This invariably takes place when the semen is retained. Another very common result is the devitalization of the veins of the spermatic cord and testicles, producing a varicose condition of the veins—varicocele and circocele.

Atrophy, or wasting away of the testicles, is also a very common sequel. This condition may take place at any period. If the practice has been commenced in early life, they do not attain their natural size, and even lose the power of secreting semen, and thus manhood is gone forever. This effect is not on the testicle alone, but upon the whole body, which is bent downward, dwarfed and robbed of its proper proportions—a perfect arrest of any further development. But this subject is inexhaustible, and we cannot go farther into detail, only to say that the critical period of life in this disease is about the time of puberty, which varies from the age of fifteen to eighteen, when the very rapid growth of the generative organs, the increased power and frequent erections cause the act, which is sure to occasion the deepest remorse. It is the attention and deliberate condition of these facts that explain to us how the habitual exercise of the genital organs, either by coition or by masturbation, may so far get control of the will of the individual. It is about this time in life when parents, through an ignorant education combined with a false modesty, have failed to do their duty by not taking the precaution to make confidents of their boys and girls by talking to them and explaining to their young minds the dangerous period their lives have about and are approaching, by warning them against such a pernicious, loathsome habit. Parents, we warn you, see that you do your duty, and be ever vigilant and on the watch, before your promising sons are ruined and sent to the mad-house. Do you not know that, according to the statistical evidence we have, three-fourths of the inmates of our insane asylums are the victims of masturbation? But we cannot follow this subject longer. But we wish we had a voice sufficiently loud that the whole world might hear our warning upon this subject.

REMEDY.—First, the habit must at once and forever be abandoned. Without this there is no available remedy. There must be strict attention paid to the general health; good nutritious diet—beef, mutton, fish, eggs, fruit and vegetables. Next, the *mind* must be under complete moral control. You must not think about such things. Get interested in some book, and dwell upon the subject. Seek the society of intelligent, cultured men and women. You should become interested in the stern realities and practicabilities of life. Then, and not till then, is there any hope for you.

Through the day take the following prescription:

Fluid extract of Xanthoxylum (prickly ash berries), one drachm;

Fluid extract of Gelsemium, half drachm.

Fluid extract of Hydrastis canad., twenty drops;
Tincture of Nux vomica, half drachm;
Glycerine, four ounces.
Mix.

Teaspoonful every three hours during the day time.

If there be nightly dreams, followed by emissions of semen, use the following prescription:

Bromide of potassa, three and one-half drachms;
Hydrate of chloral, three drachms;
Lemon syrup, three and one-half ounces.
Mix.

Dose, teaspoonful on going to bed; remember, don't take any more than this amount, unless you find you do not sleep sound; in that case, take one and one-half teaspoonfuls; take it at night only.

HOMŒOPATHIC TREATMENT.

Every function, when in healthy action, is a fountain of life and energy to all the rest of the system. Thus, the healthy soul gives strength and beauty to the body; the brain showers down its energy upon the organic system; the organic system nourishes all the organs of animal life; and in the same way the generative powers give force and spirit to every organ of the body and every passion of the soul. It is like the mutual interpenetration and influence of the elements of nature.

But when a function is diseased it brings pain, disorder and weakness to every other. Poison the brain, and the whole system reels; let disease attack the stomach or intestines, and life trembles; exhaust or disorder in any way the generative function, and the whole being suffers. Masturbation, or the solitary indulgence of amativeness, is rather a cause than a disease, and is common to both sexes, and those who practice it are more unfortunate than guilty. Inheriting an excess of passionate desire, they fall into this habit, unconscious of its evil effects. It is an act against nature; not against reason and conscience, and it brings its own punishment. Nature cannot forgive such acts; they are unpardonable. There is no reason or conscience to govern a child a few years old, and many such fall into this habit. In such cases, no doubt the disease is hereditary. A diseased parent has impressed the full force of his sensual passions upon his child. A mother marks her infant with this vice, by having her own amativeness excited during the sacred period of gestation. This is not always the cause. In little girls it comes by some accident of some uncleanliness, or eruption, irritating the parts, and compelling the friction, which results in the unnatural gratification. Boys are often abused by ignorant nurses, who play with their organs, both to gratify their own sensuality and to keep them quiet or please

them when they are peevish and fretful. Older
children, allowed to sleep with servants or children
already corrupted, are initiated into this practice.
The desire grows by gratification, and the act is
accomplished, and indulged in several times a day.
Boys usually perform the act with the hand; still
they often resort to other means. Girls have several methods or instruments they use. It is considered to be more common with girls than boys.
If this habit of self-pollution be indulged in for
any length of time, in boys it will result in involuntary seminal emission, which in itself is a disease, and a continued cause of nervous exhaustion
and final impotency. In girls it causes Leucorrhea,
or mucous discharge from the vagina, falling of
the womb, irregular and painful menstruation; a
loss of all pleasure in the sexual relation, difficult
and painful child-birth, and a whole train of nervous and hysterical affections, which make the
lives of women a burden to themselves and to all
around them.

How shall we cure this diseased manifestation,
and prevent all these horrible consequences, from
which civilization suffers from center to circumfer-
ence? Prevention is the all-important thing. Who
is responsible? Parents alone, or those in authority. Every man and woman should endeavor to
have such perfect control over their own amative
propensities and manifestation as to avoid giving

their children the terrible inheritance of diseased
and disordered passions. There is no violation of
nature which brings not its penalty. It is the
highest duty of parent, nurse, and teacher to watch
over the child from its infancy with the utmost
care. As soon as the child is old enough to understand any subject whatever, it should be taught
by its parents the uses and laws of the generative
function. Were it possible to keep children in ignorance, where can be the use? But it is not. The
animals and insects will be their teachers. They
will learn enough of evil, but not enough of good.
A true, pure, thorough knowledge should be taught
them from the first. We have seen children who
were early educated in this direction, and none
have been more modest, pure, or more capable
of taking care of themselves. Depend upon it,
parents or guardians, the best and only safeguard
to chastity is knowledge. Thousands of innocent
little ones are ruined from sheer ignorance. The
boy who has been early instructed is warned and
armed against it. The girl who understands herself and the laws that govern her being will never
plunge into solitary debauchery, nor would she be
seduced, as the ignorant girl who falls a victim to
some artful man in a moment of passionate weakness before she knows what she is doing. Be as-
sured that knowledge is the best safeguard to purity. This should not be done hastily or harshly;

explain lovingly to the child or youth all the un-
naturalness and evil consequences of this vice.
Encourage them by every motive of hope, and terror of man and womanhood, and principle, to overcome it. Give full enjoyment to mind and body,
plenty of exercise in the open air, and constant society. Much more might be said upon this subject,
but we feel enough has been said, that any thinking mind may understand the necessity of reformation in this direction. Therefore, we will proceed to give the treatment: The most important of
all is a close observance of the laws of life and
health, by diet, exercise and plenty of nature's best
remedy, that is, fresh air and pleasant surroundings.

Added to this we will give some of our best internal remedies to assist, but it should be remembered that medicine alone will not perfect a cure.

Iris. virs. 3.x.—Spermatorrhea; with pale face,
sunken eyes, depression of spirits, heavy, dragging
gait, and excitable sexual desire, nocturnal emissions, amorous dreams, confusion of mind, great
mental depression.

Kali. brom. 3.x.—Nocturnal emissions, amorous
dreams, excessive desire, constant erections at
night, profound melancholy, loss of memory.

China. 3.x.—Impotence; with lascivious fancies,
frequent and debilitating nocturnal emissions, consequences of excessive or long continued sexual
abuse.

Capsicum 3.x.—Coldness of scrotum, with impotency, atrophy of testes, shriveled spermatic cord.

Ham. 3.x.—Amorous dreams, pain in lumbar region, great prostration, severe neuralgic pain in testicle, suddenly changing to the bowels and stomach, causing nausea and faintness; profuse cold sweat at the scrotum at night. Following this, give Caladium Ustilago; Terebinthia; 10 drops to half glass of water. Teaspoonful as often as required. For great nervous prostration and debility, Cal. carb. 3.x., Phos. acid, Nitr. acid, Natr. mur., Nux vom., Gels., Puls., Graph. Prepare and give in the usual way, as symptoms indicate.

GONORRHEA.

This is a term applied to inflammation of the mucous membrane of the urethra, generally beginning at the anterior portion, attended with a contagious mucus, or muco-purulent discharge. The cause is a specific virus of veneral matter coming in contact with the part. Still, leuchorrhea, menstrual discharge, strains or blows may excite a mild type of inflammation, which will pass off in a few days. But true gonorrhea is due to the action of a specific poison depressing the part. It may be a poison of low intensity, or it may be one of great intensity; both forms produce gonorrhea.

The symptoms of both grades are identical—no true distinctive mark. Scratch the thigh of the patient and apply a little of the puss; the character of the sore so produced will reveal the type of the virus, the grade of poison. The period of incubation varies from twenty-four to forty-eight hours after illicit intercourse, sometimes longer, varying with the power of vital resistance of the patient. An itching desire to urinate frequently, heat, fullness and redness of the orifice, slight, glary discharge, like the white of an egg, which soon becomes muco-purulent, great scalding during micturition, pain in the groin, irritability of the bladder, weight and dragging down of the testicles, are symptoms. However, these symptoms are liable to numerous complications, as chordee, painful erections, balanitis, hemorrhage from the urethra, retention of urine, abscesses in the groin, prostatitis, etc., etc.

TREATMENT.—This is varied. If the patient be seen early, during the first two or three days, an effort should be made at once to abate the inflammation. If possible, this should be done by injections into the urethra, after each urination, with an injection of sulphate of zinc, grains five, to sulphate of morphia, grains two, to one ounce of water.

This will kill the virus at once, after which use the following:

                Sulphate of hydrastin .... 4 grains.
                Baking soda........................... 8   "
                Distilled water .... 3 ounces.

Mix.

Inject after each urination, a few drops, say half a teaspoonful.

        Again:

                Sulphate of hydrastin................. 2 grains.
                Pulverized borax 8   "
                Distilled water 2   "

Mix.

Inject this alternately with the above. If there be painful erections (chordee), bathe the parts at once in cold water. If it be a simple case, taken in time—this is all the treatment required. But, in old cases it will be necessary to resort to internal treatment, at the same time the injections are being used, of the following:

                Compound syrup of stillengia......... 4 ounces.
                Balsam of copaiba.................... half ounce.
                Iodi e of potassa.................... 20 grains.
                Fluid extract of gelseminum.......... half drachm.

Mix.

Dose, teaspoonful three times a day. As soon as the discharges abate take twice a day. This your druggist will prepare for you; it is good and reliable. It takes from six days to six weeks to cure these cases, according to the condition, constitution, habits and life of the individual.

HOMŒOPATHIC TREATMENT.

Aconite in the commencement of this disease. Micturition painful, difficult, drop by drop, burning distress in the urethra.

Agnus castus.—Yellow and purulent discharge after the inflammation has subsided; there is neither sexual desire nor erection.

Cantharides. 3.x.—Tenesmus, constant desire to urinate, passing only a few drops at a time, often mixed with blood; severe chordee, involuntary erection and emissions, nimphomania.

Graphites. 2.x.–Gluey, sticky discharge at the meatus urinarius which does not drop out.

Copavia. 6.x.—Violent smell of the urine; discharge purulent, with constant desire to urinate.

Cubebæ.—Itching and burning pains in the glands penis, which is swollen and bluish red; urethra inflamed, with severe pains when urinating; urine smells like the drug.

Pulsatilla. 3.x.—Orchitis, with swelling of the scrotum from too sudden check of gonorrhea; itching, burning on inner and upper side of the prepuce, with thick yellow, or green discharges. 10 to 15 drops to half glass of water. Dose, teaspoonful every half to one or two hours.

Stimulants of all kinds are strictly forbidden while the treatment is going on, and only the most nutritious food should be allowed.

ACCIDENTS AND EMERGEN-CIES.

BURNS AND SCALDS.

1 Two tablespoonfuls of bicarbonate of soda dissolved in one pint of water. Saturate cotton cloths with this solution and keep the parts well wrapped up, the cloths constantly kept wet. The pain will soon cease and the process of healing will be rapid.

2. A liniment composed of equal parts of lime-water and linseed oil, is a superior application for burns. The lime-water alone is excellent.

3. Dissolve two ounces of alum in one pint of hot water. Saturate cotton cloths with this solution and keep the burn well wrapped in them. The pain will quickly cease and the process of healing will soon commence.

Care should be taken not to let the parts be exposed to the air one moment from the time of the first application. This can be accomplished by handling the burnt parts under the water while dressing. Burns and scalds will heal rapidly, without leaving a scar, if attended to in this manner.

When the clothing of a person catches fire, throw them on the ground, roll them in a piece of carpet, a bed quilt is still better. This will extinguish the flames. If these articles are not at hand take your coat and use it instead. Begin wrapping at the neck and shoulders and wrap downwards, so as to keep the flames from the head and face. This will soon extinguish the flames; after which the burnt parts can be dressed with cosmoline. This is a new remedy, and it is an excellent one. After covering the cosmoline with one thickness of cotton cloth, wrap the entire dressing with raw cotton to exclude the air. If the weather is very warm the cosmoline dressing should be renewed twice a day; otherwise, every other day will be sufficient.

The above remedies and treatment are the best *known*, and adopted by all schools.

HOMŒOPATHIC TREATMENT.

The above is very good, and we have only to add, in very bad cases of burns and scalds some few remedies to be taken internally:

Acon. 3.x., Caust., Carb. veg., Lach., Stram., Urtic. 10 drops each to half glass of water. Dose, teaspoonful every half to one or two hours.

For external application take carbolic acid. one part to twenty of olive oil; or carron oil. equal parts lime-water and linseed oil. Keep out the air and keep the parts warm; these are two essential points in burns.

WOUNDS.

Wounds become dangerous more from their position than from their size. A small punctured wound may be more dangerous than a large cut; or, a small wound in a certain place may be more dangerous than a large one in some other spot not attended with any danger whatever. If it be dark colored blood and flows with regularity, you may be able to manage it; but if it spurts out with little jets, however small the wound may be, you must use the same means to stop it as directed in the chapter, how to stop bleeding by compress and bandage (see index), and send for your doctor at once. Cuts on the head in the hair cannot be dressed with a plaster. They may be dangerous when you do not think so.

Wounds from splinters, nails or from glass should not be closed immediately. You should let the doctor examine them.

BROKEN BONES AND DISLOCATIONS.

Of course you could not expect us to give a treatise how to remedy this difficulty; this could not be done in so small a book. We can only say that broken limbs are easily detected by the patient not being able to raise the limb, by its bending or grating sound between the joints. You may not be able to detect whether it is a dislocation, fracture or broken bone. Unless you are quite sure it is a case of dislocation you had better not undertake to jerk or pull it. Wait till the surgeon arrives, then you are on the safe side.

POISON VINE; POISON OAK.

REMEDY.—Mix a small quantity of starch with sufficient glycerine to form a thick paste and apply to the poisoned parts. This is excellent. One application is generally sufficient to affect a cure; if not, it may be repeated the following morning. This, in the author's hands, has never failed. Before the application, bathe the parts in hot water, almost hot enough to scald the flesh.

Baking soda or common washing soda will remove this difficulty very promptly by adding sufficient water to form a paste, and apply it once or twice a day. It will usually kill the poison in from two to four days.

The following is from Prof. Bundy, of Oakland, Cal., in which state poisoning is of very frequent occurrence from the poison oak. Take of the

> Fluid extract of Grindelia robusta___ 2 drachms.
> Glycerine _____ _____ 2 ounces.

Mix, and apply to the affected parts three or four times daily.

This is a new remedy, and is a specific for the poison oak poisoning; in fact, so much so that no other treatment need be mentioned. This remedy can be found at the drug stores.

HOMŒOPATHIC TREATMENT.

Agar., Arn., Corten tig., Graph., Grindelia rob., Ledum, Nymph., Sang., Sepia. Prepare and give in the usual way. For external treatment follow the above directions. They stand well recommended and can be relied upon.

SPIDER BITES.

1. Catnip and plantain (which grows in nearly everybody's dooryard), equal parts, bruised and applied to the wound, is a prompt and effectual remedy for the cure of a spider bite, or any other insect. A teaspoonful of the juice of the plantain should be taken internally every hour. This is also a cure for a hornet or bee sting. In case these remedies are not handy we will give others that are good.

2. Table salt and baking powder, equal parts, applied to the wound; this will immediately arrest the swelling and relieve the pain.

The common onion is another remedy for the same purpose, from which a piece is to be cut and at once applied. Dr. Hill uses no other remedy than this for stings, etc. If the pieces of onion are changed every few minutes the pain, he says, diminishes immediately.

ACCESSORY MEASURES.—If a wasp or other stinging insect be the cause of the trouble, examination must be made to see if the sting is left in the flesh, which is often the case. The sting must be extracted by the fingers or a pair of fine-pointed forceps.

HOMŒOPATHIC TREATMENT.

The above treatment is about all that is required in these little troubles. A few doses of Baptisia will act well as an antidote to the blood poisoning. Rest is very necessary to avoid exciting an inflammatory action in the system.

SNAKE BITES.

The first thing to do in such cases, is to arrest the circulation of the blood from the part bitten, as soon as possible. This can be done by tying a handkerchief or rope tightly around the limb, between the wound and the heart, as directed. (See chapter on Hemorrhage and How to Stop It). The wound should be sucked with all the force the patient can command, or have some person do it for him. No danger is attached to the person who does it, as long as the poison does not come in contact with any abraded or raw surface of the mouth or other parts of the body. If any considerable time has elapsed after the bite, and before the application has been made, there should be a small incision made in the flesh with a knife, across the wound, in order to more readily admit the solution, after which the bruised plantain will do good service, as before described. If that is not at hand, the next best remedy is moistened saleratus bound on the bite. Keep the parts wet with it for a few hours. This remedy has not been known to fail to cure the bite of a snake.

The old remedy is to drink plenty of good brandy till you get intoxicated; and then it sometimes fails. But it should be administered to sustain the nervous system till the poison is eliminated.

We would rather use the plantain externally and internally.

HOMŒOPATHIC TREATMENT.

Solution Fowler.—Two drops to be taken every half hour, and repeat for four hours. This, with the above treatment, is the best we know of at the present time.

SUNSTROKE.

Symptoms.—Most cases are preceded by pain in the head; wandering thoughts, or an inability to think; disturbed vision, irritability of temper, sense of pain or weight at the pit of the stomach, inability to breathe with the usual ease and satis-faction, skin dry and hot, sometimes cold, and very soon the patient feels unable to command his limbs, and finally he sinks down in a state of unconscious-ness.

Remedies.—The old method of applying cold water to the head is a bad practice, and should be abandoned.

A better method is to make warm water appli-cations. If hot water cannot be obtained bathe the head first with tepid water, and, with the hands moistened, rub the neck and whole length of the spine, then the extremities in a downward direc-tion, in order to draw the blood from the brain. As soon as hot water can be obtained, put a dry blanket around the patient, and wring flannels from the water and apply them quickly to the stomach, liver, bowels and spine. Immerse the feet in hot water, or wrap them in hot blankets. Change the flannels every eight or ten minutes for half an hour or more. Then remove them as soon as circulation is established, and apply tepid water; dry well, and rub the body briskly with the hands until a glow is produced or circulation established. As soon as the patient can swallow, give him hot water to drink and plenty of it, with occasional bits of crushed ice or a sip of cold water. Keep tepid water on the head all the time changed frequently, and all will be well in a few hours.

PREVENTION.—During the heated term the use of malt, fermented or distilled drinks should be abandoned. Wear a hat that will permit the air to pass through, and have the top lined with one thickness of flannel, or keep a damp silk handkerchief in the crown. Persons who feel the above symptoms should immediately get into the shade and bathe the head in cold water. Everything calculated to impair the strength should be avoided. Sleep is a most wonderful restorer of strength, and the want of it is often caused by a badly assorted late meal. Defective ventilation often leads to a condition of affairs favorable to the malady under consideration. Drinking large quantities of ice-cold water, particularly before and after meals, is very unwise.

HOMŒOPATHIC TREATMENT.

Bell. 3.x.—Dullness of pain, congestion of blood to the head, with whizzing in the ears; distensive headache, worse when stooping; great anguish, tearful disposition.

Lachesis. 3.x.—Burning pressure in the head from within outward; dizziness, with paleness of the face, tendency to faint and numbness; cadaverous, sunken expression, coldness of the extremities, excessive dryness of the throat, with tightness and oppression of the chest.

Camphora. 3.x.—Severe headache, congestion of the brain, fainting, delirium, convulsions, skin icy cold and covered with a cold sweat, sinking of vital forces, embarrassed respiration and circulation, tremors, cramps in the muscles.

Cactus. grand. 3.x.—Congestion to brain, blood-shot eyes, coma suffocation, flushes in the face, pulsation in temples, as if skull would burst; dimness of sight, prostration, general weakness, difficult breathing, as if an iron band prevented motion to the chest.

Glonoin. 2.x.—Distension of cerebral capillaries, reflux of blood impeded, loss of consciousness, fainting, relaxation of muscles, painful constriction of heart, etc., etc.

Veratrum viride. 3.x.—Fullness of head, throbbing arteries, increased sensitiveness to sound, buzzing in the ears, double or partial vision, rapid respiration, and dull, burning sensation in the cardiac region, faintness and blindness from sudden motion, coldness of the whole body, cold sweat on the face, hands and feet.   10 drops of each in half glass of water.   Dose, teaspoonful every hour or two, as the case may require.

HEMORRHAGE.

BLEEDING, AND HOW TO STOP IT.

Many a fond mother has had a terrible fright occasioned by her child running in with its face and clothes all smeared with blood.   It is astonishing what a big show a very little blood will make. But then it is no wonder that bleeding produces fright; animals will instinctively rush to the spot where one of their kind is bleeding to death. Blood is the life, and where there is much loss of it life is endangered.   A full knowledge of the entire structure of the body should be acquired by everyone.   It is to be hoped that this will be one of the fundamental branches taught in our public schools at no distant day.   And all should be as familiar with the bones, their structure and uses, the blood vessels, their origin and course, as they are with the rivers and lakes of the country; for no one can afford to be ignorant of the situation of the blood vessels; because some day, in the course of their lives, it may be a question with them of life and death, or some one of their friends. Accidents may happen to anyone. If the body be torn, cut or injured in any way, some one of the important blood vessels may be involved, and death may be the result in a very few moments, simply because no one present may have obtained the knowledge they might have possessed with very little study. Therefore, it is very hard for us to give rules to stop bleeding, for we do not expect everyone who reads this book to understand anatomy. We cannot tell you as we would were you acquainted with the circulatory system; yet if you will follow us we will try and give you a fair understanding of it.

BLEEDING FROM THE NOSE.

Occasionally we find a person bleeding from the nose, which is quite troublesome. The cause is generally concealed in the nervous system—*dibility* of the nervous system. Loss of nerve force is the usual cause of hemorrhage, whether from the lungs, nose, stomach, anus, or other parts of the body. Therefore, the true remedy consists in whatever restores vigor to the nervous system. Hamamelis (witch hazel) bark, or pulverized borax applied within the nostrils will stop the bleeding very soon. In the meantime cold water should be poured upon the wrists and back of the neck until the parts are very much reduced in temperature, thus arresting the rush of blood to the head. If you feel that the bleeding is going to commence, press on the large veins on either side of the throat, rubbing downwards gently.

BLEEDING ABOVE THE EAR.

If there is a wound above the ear, on either side of the head, place your finger about a quarter of an inch in front of the ear, upon the side injured, and press hard with your finger, as this point will be on the blood vessel that carries the blood from the heart up along the temple to the side of the head.

BLEEDING BELOW THE EYES.

All of the small *arteries* that carry the blood to the outside of the face, nose, lips and muscles of the face, spring from the main artery that passes over the under jaw about half-way from the angle to the point of the chin. Therefore, if you place a nickel on your thumb over the lower edge of the jawbone you will at once arrest the bleeding.

BLEEDING FROM A WOUND IN AN ARM.

Grasp the arm about two inches below the arm-pit; press tightly upon that portion which lies next to the body and a little in front of the center of the arm-pit. Or you can make a roll or pad and place it on the artery at this point, and tie a handkerchief around the part tightly, just below the arm-pit. Treated in this way the bleeding *below* this point can be checked until you send for your physician to tie the artery and dress the wound properly.

BLEEDING FROM WOUNDS IN THE LEG OR FOOT.

Lie down and support the limb above the head of the body. Then press upon the large artery which lies in front of the thigh, about mid-way of the leg, just below the groin. Fix a roll or pad (as directed to fix the pad to stop bleeding of the arm), or if you are in the field by yourself, and should get a severe cut with the scythe or other sharp instrument, take a handful of dry earth and clasp it to the wound and hold it tightly with the hand until you can get assistance.

BLEEDING FROM THE STOMACH.

It is frightful to see any one vomiting blood, and is quite dangerous, but not always as much so as it appears. Sometimes it is a question whether it be from the stomach or lungs. The blood from the stomach is darker in color than that from the lungs, and is frequently mixed with food stringy and ropy.

REMEDY.—Give two teaspoonfuls of vinegar, or lemon juice, in a little cold water, and repeat it

14

every half hour till the bleeding stops, or till your physician comes. You can also give a little cracked ice, if you have it, and nothing more, unless you understand medicine.

BLEEDING FROM THE LUNGS.

You will know the blood is from the lungs from its being coughed up instead of vomited; besides it is scarlet instead of a dark color, like that from the stomach, and is frothy in its nature. Keep the shoulders raised pretty high by pillows; sponge the chest with cold water and a little vinegar; make no exertion by talking; keep quiet; give the patient a little salt, half a teaspoonful at a dose, taken dry, and repeat often in small doses. These are the only means at hand used by the common people, and many times are the best when they do the work. The other agents belong to the doctor, and require an education and experience to use them successfully and with safety.

HOMŒOPATHIC TREATMENT.

For hemorrhage from the lungs, little can be said in addition to the above. Either of the following remedies may be used:

Acon. 3.x., Ham., Lycopus, China, Nitr. acid, Arnica, Bell., Cactus, Carbo. veg., Dulc., Ipec.

Prepare in the usual way, and give according to severity of the case.

BATH.

Baths are used both in health and disease. Bathing or sponging is indispensable; for cleanliness is next to godliness. Wash the skin all over at least twice a week. Use a little Castile soap, and then rub dry with a rough towel, having the room the right temperature to suit the condition of the patient.

Some convenient apparatus should be kept in every dwelling for bathing purposes. On the following page see cut of our combination bath apparatus, with full description of how it is made; also directions for giving the many different kinds of baths that can be administered. We shall not attempt to give a detailed description of the different baths that have been brought to notice by the hydropathic system of treatment, or any other school. Our apparatus for bathing will take the place of all other baths in use, excepting cases where patients are too feeble, then the sponge bath must be used. For these, full directions will be given under the head of Fevers.

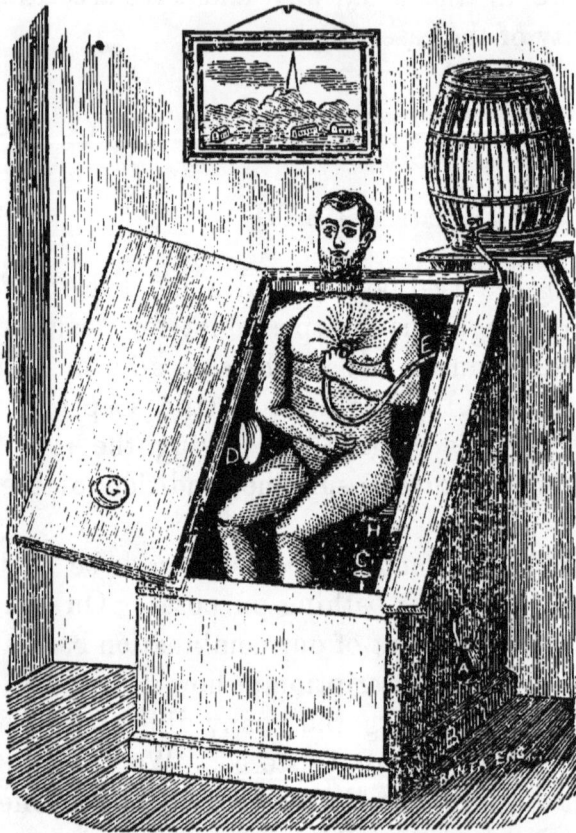

DR. BARRINGTON'S HOME TURKISH BATH.

The following dimensions will show how each family can make a Turkish bath of their own at a trifling expense, from lumber that is plowed and grooved, five-eighths of an inch in thickness:

Four feet high, 3 feet 6 inches long, 2 feet 3

inches wide—all inside measurement; 18 inches high in front up to the door; 8 inches from the back of the bath to the edge of the hole which receives the neck; hole for the neck, 5 inches in diameter; from the edge of the hole in front to the door, 6 inches—this will give you the slant of the door. There must be a slot cut in front of the hole 5 inches wide, so that when the bather seats himself in the bath box his neck can go through this slot to the hole prepared for the neck; this slot must be fitted in after the bather is in position with a block, with tongue and groove, so when it is slipped to its place it will fit the neck nicely. Then you can shut the door, and all is in readiness to proceed with your bath.

The water tank should be as high up and as far away from the bath box as convenient, so as to get the fall or force from the water through the spray, which should strike the bather with as much force as he can bear. However, all can see at a glance the bath box, bather, water tank, and faucet with hose attached, without any further description.

II represents the seat, a stool which is made to raise or lower at will. D, small slide door, in front of which, on the outside of the bath box, is a small shelf attached to hold soap, sponge, brush, and such things as the bather will need, and, by pushing back the slide door, he can help himself at will when he takes a bath without an attendant. G, slide in the main door, through which to pour additional hot water in the foot bath when required. A, slide door to admit the alcohol lamp under the patient when you want to take an alcoholic sweat, or Turkish bath, as it is called. E, India rubber hose, which is attached to the water tank; on the other end is attached a very finely punctured spray nozzle, which can be procured at the plumber's or gas-fitter's. C, stop-cock to let the waste-water run away into the waste-pipe or drain. B, iron pan, large enough to set the bath box inside of it, to catch the water in case you desire to give an invalid a bath in a bed chamber or on a parlor carpet.

This is a portable bath, and costs but little to build. Any one can see at a glance the practicability of such an arrangement. For cleansing purposes it is unequaled, as the bather can rinse himself as much or as long as he chooses; or he can sit down on a low stool, shut himself up in the bath, and spray himself, the water running on him in imitation of a shower of rain, running off in the waste-pipe. In this way you get more benefit from the water than to lie down in it; therefore it is more scientific.

Besides all these advantages, we have a combination bath-tub all in one. We can give a better Turkish bath at your own home than you can get in any large city; inasmuch as many cannot stand the hot air on their heads, you can take the hot air sweat with the head outside of the box; or, you can sit on a low stool, shut the bath box, and in this way you have the real Turkish bath, only better in every way. Then you can give the vapor bath, the electrical bath, the sulphur fume bath, and the medicated vapor bath, all in this one box, each of which can be followed by the spray. The water can be warmed and prepared previous to taking the bath.

ALCOHOL SWEAT BATH.

First, we must describe the alcohol lamp, which should be used for this purpose, and no other kind. The lamp should not be more than two inches high, sufficiently large to hold half a pint of alcohol; the tube for the wick should also be two inches high and large enough to hold a wick that is $\frac{3}{4}$ of an inch in diameter; the wick should be twisted into this tube as tight as possible. There should be a place to pour in the alcohol, made with a screw, like the top of a kerosene can; this large size wick will give heat enough to produce sufficient perspiration in a very short time. After adjusting yourself on the stool in the bath box, your feet placed in hot water, light the lamp and place it in front of you in the corner of the bath tub; shut the door, and the process of the bath begins. You can sweat 25 or 30 minutes; occasionally add more hot water to the foot bath; if you should feel too hot during the process of the sweat, you can open the bath door occasionally and let in the cool air. In this case, you will have to prolong the sweat from 40 to 50 minutes, after which take out your lamp and turn on the water through the hose pipe and spray yourself just a little; then shampoon your body all over with soap; then spray yourself again, rub dry with a towel. This kind of bath taken once a week will preserve your health without resorting to drugs of any kind; if you are sick, it is the quickest way to effect a cure. It is safe to repeat every day if necessary, only the sweat is not continued longer than 15 minutes.

TURKISH BATH.

This bath is taken the same as the above, with this exception, the patient can sit on a low stool; and when the bath door is shut the patient will be inclosed inside the box, head and all; in this way they breathe the hot air directly into the lungs. Remain in 15 or 20 minutes, or longer if necessary, after which the spraying and shampooning begins the same as described above. This completes the bath.

MEDICATED BATH.

This is given in the same way as the Turkish bath, with this difference, the medicine which you choose to use is placed in a vessel with one

pint of water added; this should sit on a stand sufficiently high to allow your lamp to be placed
under it that it may be kept boiling, so the steam
or vapor arising therefrom may be inhaled into the
lungs by the patient, at the same time they are
having a good sweat. Then comes the spray as
before; you then have a combination of three baths
in one. Time required for the sweat is from 15 to
50 minutes, according to the constitution and condition of the patient. This will soon become ap-
parent after a few baths are taken. For consumptive patients, catarrh, bronchial difficulty, or sudden cold in the head or lungs this bath is called for
and is excellent. The medicines used for such purposes are the lobelia and pennyroyal herbs. Quantity for one bath; take as much as you can hold
with the thumb and two fingers of the lobelia and
twice that quantity of the pennyroyal to one pint
of boiling water. Other remedies are often used
and can be prescribed by your physician to meet
the indications, but these two herbs are sufficient
for all ordinary purposes.

SULPHUR FUME BATH.

Take either one of the above-named baths after
the sweat is about half through; take an iron vessel of any kind, fire-shovel will do; heat it sufficiently hot to burn the flour of sulphur, so as to
produce a fume; put this hot iron in your bath

tub, and sprinkle about a teaspoonful of the flour of sulphur upon it; shut the bath box as quick as possible and cover the outside with a sheet, to prevent the sulphur fumes from escaping into the room; remain in this fume for 12 or 15 minutes, then get out and go into another room quickly, and remain there till some one opens the doors and windows of the room and lets the sulphur escape; then you can return and finish your bath, by shampooing and spraying the body thoroughly.

HOW TO BATHE THE BABY.

The best way to bathe the baby when sick is to take a small blanket, wrung from tepid water, spread it over the mother's lap, lay the little one in her arms, well wrapt in the wet blanket, this being snugly covered with a dry one, to protect it from the cold air; the baby should remain in this position from 30 to 40 minutes, then remove the blankets and sponge off with tepid water, rubbing briskly with a dry towel; place it in a warm, dry sheet, with sufficient covering to keep the little one comfortable. Usually a sweet, restful sleep follows, which is nature's best restorer, and the baby wakens much refreshed. This method can be repeated several times, if desired, with perfect safety, and proves very efficient in many of the ills that are incident to children. But it should always be remembered that the room should be kept warm, and no draft from doors or windows while administering the bath.

FOOT BATH.

This bath is very necessary for many purposes—for headache, sudden cold, etc. It is usually taken on going to bed. The water should be as hot as could be borne; place the feet in it, and throw a blanket over the limbs to retain the heat; let them remain 20 or 30 minutes, or longer, if desired. As the water cools, more hot should be added. If the patient is troubled with cold feet, add a tablespoonful of ground mustard with the water. If you wish to sweat after the bath, you should drink hot teas, such as ginger, smart weed, or a hot lemonade, with a little whisky or capsicum (red pepper) added; retire immediately, place hot irons to the feet, and cover up well, until free perspiration is produced.

HIP, OR SITZ BATH.

Sufficient water should be placed in a tub to cover the hips and lower portion of the abdomen. When the patient is in a sitting posture the water can be made any temperature to suit the immediate indications. The patient should remain in the bath the length of time indicated by the physician. Most all physicians prescribe this bath for various diseases. We would add in case of painful or suppressed menses this bath is very good. Sometimes we order this and the foot bath together.

RECIPES, ETC.

CONSTIPATION OF THE BOWELS.

AN INFALLIBLE PRESCRIPTION.

Fluid extract of Cascara sagrada, one ounce.
Fluid extract of Grindelia squarrosa.
Fluid extract of Podophyllum peltatum.
Tincture of Nux vomica, of each one-half drachm.
Glycerine, two and one-half ounces.
Mix.
Dose, teaspoonful after each meal and on going to bed.

This medicine acts slow at first, but when once its action takes place, then less quantity is required —taken once or twice a day, or once every other day; it should be taken regularly enough to have the bowels move under its influence, till the medicine is all taken. This will cure persistent cases of constipation effectually as no other prescription ever has. It is invaluable, and is worth more than the price of a dozen books like this. The fluid extract of Cascara sagrada of Park, Davis & Co.'s manufacture is also a good preparation. The cascara is good for dyspepsia; taken in small doses we

consider this one of the most valuable remedies
ever given to medical science.

DR. BARRINGTON'S RESTORATIVE COM-
POUND.

FOR INTERNAL OR EXTERNAL USE.

Good for cholera morbus, nervous headache, and
all kinds of relaxed conditions of the bowels:
Oil of organium.
Oil of sassafras, of each one ounce.
Pure sweet spirits of nitre, three ounces.
Saturated tincture of camphor, one ounce.
Essence of peppermint, two drachms.
Fluid extract of capsicum, one drachm.
Chloroform, three ounces.
Aqua ammonia, fff, two ounces.
Ninety-eight per cent. alcohol, half a pint.
Mix, and keep well corked.
For sprains, bruises, rheumatism, or weak back,
bathe the parts well with the medicine, applied
with the hands.
To treat a case of cholera, the medicine takes
the place of a mustard draft, by wetting the hand
and laying it on the stomach, wrists and soles
of the feet, taking care to hold the hand still, ex-
cluding all the air where it is applied; give a half

teaspoonful internally every ten or fifteen minutes, as directed for internal use; bathe the body all over with the medicine, rub with the hands till the body smarts or feels hot; then cover the patient with a dry, hot blanket.

For nervous sick headache, bathe the temples, back of the ears and neck, and on top of the head. Smell occasionally, and take half a teaspoonful every ten or fifteen minutes.

FOR INTERNAL USE.

This medicine should be prepared as follows:

To one teaspoonful of the medicine add two of water; mix in a tumbler, stir well; it should be mixed as it is used, as it loses its qualities by exposure to the air. Keep the bottle well corked.

For chronic diarrhea—Dose, one teaspoonful to one and a half, as the case requires, every half hour to four and six hours.

For children, the medicine should be weakened by adding more water and a little sugar, according to the age of the child, and as your judgment dictates.

N. B.—Remember, this medicine must never be taken *internally full strength*, it will burn the stomach.

This medicine is invaluable, and should be kept in every family. The author has saved the life of

many with this prescription. It is the most valuable medicine in all such cases, and is in great demand wherever the author is known.

COUGH SYRUPS.

There are many kinds of coughs that arise from
many causes; we give you a formula you can always
vary to meet the indications. However, you should
remember, a syrup made from spices, cloves, cínna-
mon, allspice, cardamon seed, etc., is always called
for in a cough arising from any cause. This you
can make yourself and keep on hand, add a little
of this to your cough syrup, just sufficient to flavor
it. We call this No. 1.

BALSAM FOR WEAK LUNGS—NO. 2.

Oil of sweet almonds, one ounce.
Gum Arabic, dissolved, one ounce.
Tincture of horehound, one ounce.
Tincture of Jamaica ginger, one-half ounce.
Syrup of stillingia, two ounces.
Syrup of honey, one ounce.
Good brandy, two ounces.
Mix.
Now you can add about an ounce of No. 1 to
this, sufficient to make a ten-ounce mixture.
Dose, half a teaspoonful every half hour till the

cough is better, then prolong the intervals to one, two, or three hours.

COUGHS FROM COLDS, WITH SORE LUNGS—NO. 3.

Fluid extract of asclepias tub. (pleurisy root).

Fluid extract of lycopus virg. (sweet bugle weed).

Fluid extract of collinsonia (stone root), of each one drachm.

Tincture of lobelia seed, twenty drops.

Tincture of ipecac, one-half drachm.

Syrup of horehound, one ounce.

Syrup of stillingia, two ounces.

Good brandy, one ounce.

Mix.

Add one-half ounce of No. 1.

Dose, teaspoonful every hour or two; for children, reduce accordingly.

If either of these remedies are too strong they can be reduced with a little water, or the juice of one lemon and water, to suit the taste. Your druggist can put them up for you, and they will keep for years.

NOTE.—The crab apple stewed, the juice strained and added to either of the above cough syrups, after sweetening to the taste is excellent for all bronchial trouble. Then you have the finest cough medicines ever used.

HOMŒOPATHIC.—Coughs usually arise from some diseased condition of the system; there are many kinds and as many causes; special remedies are called for. The following will reach the leading indications:

For dry cough without expectoration:—Aconite, Arum., Bell., Bry., •Cal. carb., Cham., Hyos., Ign., Ipec., Iris ver., Lach., Nux vom., Phos., Spong., Sulphur. 2d. Hepar sulph., Arn., Ars., Ant., Carb. v., Ferr., Kali. bic., Chin., Cup., Spig., Squill, Lobe.

For loose cough with expectoration:—Ars., Cal. carb., China, Bry., Iod., Phos., Puls., Sepa., Sil., Squill, Sulph., Ferr., Lept., Eupt. pur., Hydr., Collins.

For hoarse, deep cough:—1st. Aconite, Bell., Bry., Hep., Sulph., China, Ign., Murc. sol., Nux v., Sticta pulm. 2d. Acon., Ambr., Apoc. can., Arsen., Cal. carb., Caust., Kreos., Lyc., Nitr. ac., Phyto., Sabin.

For barking, exhaustive cough:—1st. Aconite, Ars., Bell., Lach., Lob. infl., Merc. cor., Nux vom., Puls., Stram., Sulph. 2d. Arsen., Anac. orient., Carb. veg., Hoyoc., Gymnoc can., Ign., Lyc., Sil., Ipec. Prepare and take in the usual way. Use 3.x.

DYSENTERY—BLOODY FLUX.

Fluid extract of chamomile, one drachm.

Fluid extract of epilobium (" wake up willow " herb), one drachm.

15

Fluid extract of Crocus satava (saffron), one drachm.

Fluid extract of Polygala seneca (seneca snake root), two drachms.

Camphor gum, five grains.

Pulverized opium, twenty grains.

Best brandy, two ounces.

(Dissolve the opium and camphor first in the brandy).

Syrup of ginger.

Syrup of lemon, of each sufficient to make six ounces.

Mix. Shake well.

Dose: For a child of one year or under, from four to six drops, in a little sweetened water; two years old, from eight to ten drops; four years old, twenty drops; adults, from one to one and one-half tea-spoonfuls every half hour to four and six hours apart, as the case demands.

This is a sure cure for bloody flux, diarrhea, and all relaxed conditions of the bowels. We never knew it to fail in a single case where there were no other complications. But should there be inflammation of the bowels, you should put the patient on oatmeal water or slippery elm for a drink; injections of the same are necessary. Diet, extract of beef, milk punch, etc., See page 17 and 22.

HOMŒOPATHIC.—The above prescription we have tried, and with marked success; it may be given in homœopathic doses if desired, using a teaspoonful to half glass of water, giving teaspoonful every half hour in severe cases; as the patient is relieved prolong the intervals.

We also add some of our remedies:

1st. Acon., Aloes, Arn., Arsen., Bapt., Ham., Iris. ver., Merc. cor., Rhus., Sulph. Alternate these if desired. 2d. Bry., Carb. veg., China, Collins., Nux. vom., Gels., Diosco., Geran., Hydras. 3.x. Prepare and administer in the usual way.

LOSS OF APPETITE.

Tincture of Apocynum canabinum (Indian hemp) half drachm.

Tincture of Hydrastis canad., one drachm.

Elixir of vitriol, three drachms.

Simple syrup, four ounces.

Mix.

Dose, teaspoonful after each meal.

Nux. vom., Hydr. can., Ferr., Met., Phos. acid., Iris. ver., Cal. carb., Puls., 3.x.; 10 drops to half glass of water.

Dose, teaspoonful every one or two hours. Alternate each remedy every day.

EXCESS OF VOMITING.

Tincture of nux vomica, from two to five drops.
Tincture of ipecac, from ten to fifteen drops.
Water, four ounces.
Mix.
Dose, teaspoonful every half hour.
Also, a weak decoction of peach, or apple tree
leaves, taken alternately with the above will do
the work.   •
Homœopathic.—Hematemesis (vomitus cruen-
tus). 1st. Aconite nap., Aloes, Arn., Ars., Ferr.
met., Hyoc., Ipec., Nux vom., Phos. 2d. Amm.,
Bell., Canth., Carb. veg., Caust., Chin., Lych.,
Plumb., Alum., 3.x. Alternate and take them every
10 or 20 minutes till relieved, then prolong the
intervals.

EARACHE.

Glycerine of tannin, half ounce.
Tincture of laudanum, twenty drops.
Sulphate of hydrastin, two grains.
Sulphuric ether, one drachm.
Mix.
Drop three or four drops of this medicine in the
ear, from off the end of a little stick is the best.
We have never known this to fail in a single in-

stance to cure this distressing disease in children in a very few minutes.

HOMŒOPATHIC.—We claim if the system be in good condition there will be no need of local application, and they sometimes prove injurious to the internal organs that may result in permanent deafness.

INACTION OF THE KIDNEYS.

Fluid extract of Eupatorium purpureum (queen of the meadow), one-half ounce.

Fluid extract of Asclepias tub. (pleurisy root), one drachm.

Fluid extract of Sanguinaria cana (blood root), twenty drops.

Nitrate of potass., two and a half drachms.

Syrup of lemon.

Syrup of ginger, of each two ounces.

Mix.

Dose, teaspoonful every three hours.

This prescription is excellent following rheumatism or malarial fevers to free the poison in the blood and carry it out of the system through the kidneys.

HOMŒOPATHIC.—Nephritis Retinitis.—If there is retention, or scanty urination; Apis., Ars., Gels., Bell., Phos. ac., Salicyl. acid., Sep., Dulc., Lyc.,

Canth., Urtic., Chloral, Ustilago maidis, Eupa. pur., 3.x. Prepare and give in the usual way.

SUMMER DIARRHEA IN LITTLE CHILDREN.

From eighteen months to five years old give
Sugar of milk, one-half ounce.
Lactopeptine, fifteen grains.
Hydrochloric acid.
Lactic acid, of each one-half drachm.
Tincture of Xanthoxylum (prickly ash berries), one drachm.
Syrup of lemon.
Water, of each one ounce.
Mix.

Dose, teaspoonful every hour, or half a teaspoonful every half hour is better; as the symptoms improve prolong the intervals.

HOMŒOPATHIC.—If child does not thrive or sleep well, Cham., China, Nux. v., Cal. carb., Iris. ver. Cholera infantum, vomiting, Cal. carb. (curded sour milk), Sil., Ars., Phos., Ant. crud. Vomits green curd, exhausted afterwards, Kreosote. (Diarrhea, indigested food), Sulph., Cal. carb. (Contains curdled mild), Graph., (if thin, brown, half-digested and fetid), Phos., (if hot), Camphor. (With great exhaustion), Phos. acid, Hepar sul. (If sour, white or green), Ant. crude. (Hard lumps of curdled milk), Ipec., Nux v. (Stools changeable, very offensive), Cal. carb., Carbo. veg., Gels., Nux v., Hydr., Ipec., Podo., Lept. (Cold sweat), Verat. alb. Prepare and give in the usual way.

CATARRH OF THE BLADDER.

The common Ustilago maidis or rhus aromatica (skunk bush).

Fluid extract, of Park, Davis & Co.'s manufacture.

Teaspoonful at a dose, in a little sweetened water, three or four times a day; as the symptoms improve prolong the intervals.

For insipidus (diabetes)—children wetting the bed—take

Rhus aromatica, one ounce.

Glycerine, two ounces.

Water, one ounce.

Mix.

Dose, teaspoonful every three or four hours, as the case demands.

This is a new remedy, introduced to the profession by Dr. McClanahan. He says for bladder troubles this remedy surpasses all others. It has been well endorsed by many other eminent physicians as accomplishing all that Dr. McClanahan claims for it. We have had no case nor occasion to try it.

HOMŒOPATHIC.—First. Colch., Dulc., Lyc., Nux v., Puls., Sulph. Second. Ant., Apis., Bell., Ergot., Apoc. can., Cal. carb., Carbo. veg. If blood passes with urine, give Ham., Lyco., Canth. If chronic cases, Cal. carb., Carbo. veg., Hyd., Kali., Phosph., 3.x. Prepare and take the same.

TONIC FOR DISEASE OF THE KIDNEYS.

Balsam of Fir, three ounces.

Balm of Gilead buds, fresh ones, two ounces.

Linn bark, one ounce.

Steep the buds and bark slowly in sufficient water to get the strength. Then strain and add sufficient sugar to make a pint; cut the balsam, add a pint of good Holland gin. Then add the syrup of the buds and bark, and shake well.

Dose, teaspoonful three or four times a day.

This is one of the most valuable tonics for diseases of the kidney, with constant pain in the back, we have ever used. It is invaluable.

HOMŒOPATHIC.—Aconite., Alum., Bell., Canth., Terb., Cam., Caust., China, Collins., Eupat. purp., Gels., Geran., Lyc., Nux v., Phyt., Chimaphila, Kali. carb., 3.x. Prepare and take in the usual way.

COMMON BILIOUS CONDITION.

Tincture of gelsemium,
Tincture of nux vomica, of each one drachm.
Citric acid, one-half drachm.
Sulphate of quinine, thirty grains.
Glycerine, two and one-half ounces.
Mix.
Dose, teaspoonful in a little water after each meal.

HOMŒOPATHIC.—1. Principal remedies. Apis., Ars., Chin., Eupat. pur., Ign., Ipec., Lach., Rhus., Sulph. 2. In cold, damp seasons, Cal. carb., Carbo. veg., China, Lach., Nux mosch., Puls., Rhus., Sulphur. Prevailing in spring and summer, or in warm seasons generally.—First. Ars., Bell., Calc., Caps., Chin., Ipec., Lach., Sulph., Verat.; second. Ant. crud. Bry., Carbo. veg., Natr. mur., Nux vom., Puls., Sulph. Use the 3.x.; 10 to 12 drops of each to half glass of water. Dose, teaspoonful every hour.

MALARIAL AFFECTIONS.

Tincture of iodine, ten drops in a third of a tumbler of sweetened water at one dose, three times a day, cures it better and quicker than quinine. For children, give proportionate doses.

HOMŒOPATHIC.—The remedies for this affection are nearly the same as the above, common bilious condition, unless it should be chronic or malignant; in that case, when chill is on, give, first, Acon., Bry., Caps., Carb. veg., Cham., Chin., Hep., Puls., Sabina. When chill and fever is off, give Phod., Gels., and alternate them. Second. Sep., Gels., Iris. v., China, Nux vom.—take your choice of either of the two last—3.x. Prepare and take in the usual way; continue till return of chill, then return to the first remedy under this head.

BONE FELONS, CARBUNCLES AND BOILS.

To allay the pain in these distressing comforters use the following prescription:

Tincture of aconite root,
Tincture of arnica,
Tincture of cantharides,
Tincture of veratrum, of each two drachms.
Tincture of iodine, three drachms.
Mix.

Saturate a cotton cloth and apply to the parts, and keep it wet with the mixture till the pain ceases; give twenty-drop doses of the arnica every hour.

HOW TO PREVENT A FELON.

It is unnecessary for any one to have a felon if the white of an egg and half a teaspoonful of salt is applied in time. It will scatter it at once. We have tried it many times with success. But if it is not done in time it will do no good.

The following prescription will draw it to the surface very quickly.

Take equal parts of brown soap and unslaked lime, equal parts of whisky and common kerosene, until a salve is made, bind it on the felon. In twenty-four hours it will draw the matter to the surface, when it can be removed.

DIPHTHERIA.

Dialyzed iron, two drachms.
Chlorate of potassa, one drachm.
Tincture of iodine, five drops.
Distilled water, half ounce.
Glycerine, one and one-half ounces.
Mix.

Dose, for a child five years old, half a teaspoonful in a little sweetened water, every one or two hours, as the case demands.

FOR EXTERNAL APPLICATION.

Fluid extract of belladonna, two ounces;
Hydrate of chloral, half ounce;
Glycerine, half ounce.

Dissolve the chloral in two ounces of water; mix all together. Apply on the outside of the throat with a cotton cloth, and a flannel over it.

HOMŒOPATHIC.—Gangrænosa Malignant Sore-Throat.—The best remedies are: First. Apis., Carbol. acid, Kali. bic., Lach., Phyt., Lach., Mur. cor., Nitr. ac., Salicyl. acid, Sulph. ac. Second. Bapt., Ars., Bell., Kali. brom., Mur. ac. Third. Alum., Amm. carb., Chlor. hyd., Ars., Kali. permang., Kreosote, Phosph., Arum. met., Ars. iod., 3.x. Prepare and use as usual. These classes should be alternated.

RHEUMATISM.

Iodide potassium, one-half ounce.

Solid extract of conium, two drachms.

Syrup aralia, compound of American Dispensatory, six ounces.

Mix.

Dose, teaspoonful three times a day.

Dr. Pitzer says this never fails to cure any kind of muscular rheumatism.

HOMŒOPATHIC.—For acute forms:—If swollen and inflamed, use the cotton-batten bandages, exclude the air and keep the parts warm; give Acon., Apis., Caust., Colch., Ars., Phyt., Carbo. veg., Lach., Sep., Sulph., Apoc. can., Eup. pur. Salicylate of soda, 3.x. Prepare and take in the usual way.

FOR RICKETY CHILDREN.

For little children whose muscles are flabby, the bones weak, and do not seem to grow strong, give them

Hypophosphite of lime.

Hypophosphite of potassium, of each one drachm.

Hydrochloric acid.

Fluid extract of Hydrastis (yellow root), of each one-half drachm.

Lactopeptine, one-half drachm.

Syrup of rhubarb, one-half ounce.

Syrup of lemon, three ounces.

Mix.

Dose, teaspoonful three times a day. Bathe your child in soda water; alternate with salt and water.

HOMŒOPATHIC.—Under this head we give, first. Asaf., Bell., Calc. carb., Secale, Caust., Lyc., Nitr. ac., Phos. ac., Ign., Brom. amm., Baryta. Sulph.. Silicea, Kali. phos., 3.x. Prepare and give in the usual way.

ERYSIPELAS.

Dialyzed iron, half ounce.

Tincture of iodine, ten drops.

Sulphate of quinine, twenty grains.

Glycerine, one and one-half ounces.

Mix.

Dose, half a teaspoonful in a little water every three hours.

In this disease, remember, the bowels must be kept open by cathartics, or injections of a little salt and water.

For external treatment in erysipelas, use the following prescription:

Sulphate of soda, two drachms.

Tincture of Dioscorea vil. (wild yam,)

Tincture of Veratrum vir.

Tincture of Lobelia seed, of each two drachms.

Distilled water, four ounces.

Mix.

Wet a cotton cloth in this mixture and lay it on the affected parts and keep it moist with the medicine. If the disease is on the face, care should be taken not to get any of the medicine in the eyes.

Dose, to a child of five years old, half a teaspoonful in a little sweetened water. every one or two hours, as the case demands.

HOMŒOPATHIC.——Principal remedies :——Acon., Apis., Arn., Bell., Bry., Camph., Canth., Euphorbium, Lach., Puls., Rhus., Sulph. Alternate with Borax, Salcylate of soda, Phyto., Graph., Cal. carb., Bapt., Sulph., Ferr. Prepare and give in the usual way; use the 3.x.

CHAPPED HANDS, FACE OR LIPS.

Cosmoline is the most excellent of anything we have ever used. Apply it several times a day.

RHEUMATIC GOUT.

Tincture of Iris versicolor (blue flag), three drachms;
Tincture of Xanthoxylum (prickly ash), one drachm;
Glycerine, four ounces.
Mix.
Dose, teaspoonful three times a day. Sponging and bathing the body are always called for in this disease.

HOMŒOPATHIC.—If the joints are swollen much and very painful, they should be kept warm by bandages made from cotton batten. The best remedies: First. Puls., Apo. can., Cim. rac., Bry., Rhod., Rhus., for a few days; then followed by Colch., Eup. pur., Sang. can., Sulph., Salicylate of Soda. Use the 3.x. Prepare and take in the usual way.

CONVULSIONS IN LITTLE CHILDREN.

Bromide of sodium, forty grains
Simple syrup, one-half ounce;
Camphor water, one-half ounce.
 lix.
Dose, teaspoonful every two or three hours.

For a child three years old, three grains of bromide of sodium in a little simple syrup three times a day.

HOMŒOPATHIC.—Aconite, Ambrosia, Apis., Ars., Bell., Caust., Cham., Cina., Cupr., Coff., Gels., Ign., Ipec., Kali. brom., Lach., Lachn., Lil. tigr., Nux vom., Scutel., Stram., Sulph., Vir. alb. Use the 3.x. Prepare and give in the usual way. The most simple way to bring the child out of the spasm is to force a little salt and water in its mouth; put its feet in hot water; as soon as it recovers from the convulsion give Gels. and Bell. in alternation for several hours, or perhaps days, until all symptoms have subsided.

PAINFUL MENSTRUATION.

Fluid extract Dioscorea vil. (wild yam), one and a half drachms;

Fluid extract of Gelseminum, one drachm;
Tincture of Aconite root, ten drops;
Glycerine,
Water, of each, two ounces.
Mix.
Dose, teaspoonful every hour till relieved, then prolong the intervals.

HOMŒOPATHIC.—Menstrual difficulties.—Principal remedies: Apis., Bell., Bry., Gels., Diosc. vil., Cal. carb., Cocc., Graph., Ign., Nux v., Sep., Phos., Sulph. Second. Alternate with Acon., Amm., Carb. v., Caust., Cupr., Kali., Lach., Sil., Zinc., Cham., Phos. ac., Sabina., 3.x. 10 drops in half glass of water. Dose, teaspoonful every half, one or two hours, according to severity of case. Hot application to the abdomen either wet or dry.

PROFUSE MENSTRUATION.

Fluid extract of Ergot,
Fluid extract of Hammamelis, of each one drachm;
Fluid extract of Cannabis indica (Indian hemp), two and one-half drachms;
Fluid extract of Macroty's (black cohosh), one drachm;
Glycerine, four ounces.
Mix.

16

Dose, teaspoonful every one or two hours, as the case requires, or it can be taken every half hour in urgent cases. As the symptoms improve prolong the intervals.

HOMŒOPATHIC.—Menorrhagia, Metrorrhagia.— First. Ham., Ergot., Croc., Ferr. met., Helon., Hyoc., Sab. Second. Alternate with Acon., Aletr., Cal. carb., Carb. veg., Cimicif., Ign., Apo. can., Asclep. tub., Bapt., Gels., Iris. ver., Phyto. 3.x. Prepare and give in the usual way. Perfect rest is the all-important thing during the flow; then constitutional treatment between the periods.

RHEUMATISM.

Iodide of potassa, five drachms.

Solid extract of Conium, two drachms.

Syrup of aralia (the compound of the American Dispensatory), six ounces.

Mix.

Dose, teaspoonful three or four times a day.

Dr. Pitzer says this will cure rheumatism when all other remedies fail. We have never tried it.

HOMŒOPATHIC.—We have given sufficient treatment for this disease under other headings. The most essential part is in keeping the system in good condition, that nature may have a chance to

do her work readily and promptly; by so doing,
much suffering is avoided. Good blood with active circulation will conquer nearly all ills.

CATARRH SNUFF.

Powdered bayberry root, one and one-half
drachms.

Powdered galangal root, one and one-half
drachms.

Powdered valerian, thirty-six grains.

Powdered blood root, sixteen grains.

Powdered camphor gum, fifteen grains.

Powdered burnt alum, thirty-six grains.

Mix, and triturate all together well.

Snuff a little of this up the nostrils three or four
times a day. It is the best we have ever used for
catarrh, followed by the nasal douche once a day.

CRAMPS IN THE STOMACH OR BOWELS.

OR DIAPHORETIC POWDER.

Powdered opium, ten grains.

Powdered ipecac, twenty-five grains.

Powdered camphor, forty grains.

Powdered saltpetre, two and one-half drachms.
Mix, and triturate well together.

From three to five grains at a dose; repeat if necessary, every three or four hours. Dr. Scudder says this is excellent in all such cases.

PILES—HEMORRHOIDS.

Fluid extract of Hammamelis.
Fluid extract of Ergot.
Fluid extract of Hydrastis canadensis.
Tincture of Arnica.
Tincture of Laudanum.
Simple syrup.
Distilled water, of each one ounce.
Burnt alum, one-half drachm.
Glycerine of tannin, one half ounce.
Mix.

Take a small ear syringe and inject ten or fifteen drops into the rectum; after which lie down and keep quiet; take a small tuft of cotton and saturate it with the mixture and keep it pressed up against the tumors, keep them constantly moist with the medicine for several days, or longer if required. If the medicine is too strong for the inflamed parts, it can be weakened with a little sweet oil or simple syrup and oil. This will absorb the

tumors in a very short time, as well as relieve the
pain, and perform a cure in a very short time without resorting to surgical operations or caustics.

This is the most valuable remedy ever given to
the world. The author has never failed to cure
every case he has undertaken. Ointments are useless, except the cosmoline.

INTERNAL REMEDY FOR HEMORRHOIDS.

Tincture of Æsculas hipp., (horse-chestnut).
Tincture of Phytolacca decand. (poke-root), of
each one-half ounce.

Mix.

Dose, twenty drops in half a tumbler of water;
teaspoonful every hour.

This should be taken for several days, mixing it
fresh every day.

Homœopathic.—Principal Remedies:–1st, Acon.
Æscul. hipp., Ars., Ant. crude, Bell., Cal. carb.,
Caps., Carb. v., Cham., Collins., Diosc., Ham., Ign.,
Hydr., Mur. ac., Phos. acid, Nux v. 2d, Alter-
nate with Ambr., Aloes, Amm. carb., Amm. mur.,
Causticum, Chel., Chin., Erig., Graph., Kali. bic.,
Lach., Lept., Phyto., 3.x. Prepare and take in the
usual way. With the above external application and
these remedies you may always expect prompt and
permanent relief.

NURSING SORE MOUTH.

Pure rain water, one half gallon.
Pulverized Hydrastis (yellow root), one ounce.
Burnt alum, one ounce.
Table salt, one ounce.

While you are burning the alum, and it is bubbling, sprinkle the salt over the alum. Mix all together with the juice of two lemons; let stand in the sun three or four days, shaking occasionally. Apply to the gums and ulcers with a cotton rag two or three times a day. If it is too strong, weaken with a little sugar and water.

Dr. J. Bobb says this never fails to cure these troubles.

INTERNAL MEDICINE FOR SAME.

Neutralizing cordial, of American Dispensatory, four ounces.
Fluid extract of collinsonia (stone root).
Fluid extract of Hydrastis canadensis, of each two drachms.
Fluid extract of Macroty's (black cohosh).
Fluid extract of Eupatorium aromaticum (snake root), of each one half ounce.
Mix.

Dose, teaspoonful three or four times a day. For a child, weaken accordingly.

HOMŒOPATHIC.—Close attention to ventilation and hygiene; swab the mouth often with sage tea and honey, or solution of borax-water, golden thread or Gum Arabic. A few remedies may be called for: Acon., Merc. cor., Puls., Bell., Nux vom. Prepare and give in the usual way.

NIPPLE WASH. (DR. ATTLER'S CELEBRATED.)

Powdered borax, one drachm
Gum Arabic, two drachms.
Tincture of myrrh, three drachms.
Distilled water, four ounces.
Mix.
Apply to the nipple two or three times a day.

HOMŒOPATHIC.—Bathe the nipple in tepid water before and after nursing the baby; a weak solution of arnica or hamamelis for a wash is good. Few remedies are required, Cal. carb., Ham., Sil., Sulph. Prepare and give as usual.

SPRAINS.

Take a large spoonful of honey, the same amount of salt, the white of one egg; beat the whole incessantly for two hours; let stand for one hour;

then anoint the place sprained with the oil which will be produced from the mixture. This is said to have enabled persons with sprained ankles to walk in twenty-four hours, entirely free from pain. *King.*

HEALING SALVE

One-half pound of beeswax, one-half pound of salty butter, one-quarter pound of turpentine, six ounces of the balsam of fir. Simmer slowly for half an hour, when it is ready for use.

Dr. Curtiss has used this preparation for years for old sores, wounds and burns, and has never found anything to surpass it.

RING WORM AND TETTER.

A strong tincture made from green walnut hulls, and applied externally to the ring worm. Take half a pint of alcohol and add a handful of green hulls to it, let it stand for five or six days; this is the way to get the tincture. Also, teaspoonful of this tincture added to a half tumbler of water; stir well, and take a teaspoonful every hour internally. It is advisable to take it for three or four days, making it fresh every morning.

ENLARGEMENT OF THE SPLEEN.

Fluid extract of Grindelia squarrosa (new remedy).

Fluid extract of Polymnia uvedalia (bearsfoot), of each one ounce.

Glycerine.

Distilled water, of each one ounce.

Mix.

Dose, teaspoonful every three hours.

Get your druggist to prepare it for you.

GOOD FOR THE KIDNEYS IN DROPSICAL AFFECTIONS.

Bruised Juniper berries.

Mustard seed.

Ginger, of each one-half ounce.

Bruised horse-radish.

Bruised parsley root, of each one ounce.

Old sour cider, one quart.

Let stand and infuse for several days.

Dose, wineglassfull three times a day.

This is excellent for all kidney troubles.

SURE CURE FOR BUNIONS, OR FROST-BITES.

Take the common glue, prepare it in the same way the cabinet makers do, only thicker; spread it on a piece of linen the size you want it, and apply it to the bunion as hot as can be borne; let it remain for several days, and repeat if necessary. It will do it every time.

SCURVY.

Plenty of lemon juice, sweetened to taste, cures every time. Lemon syrup, or syrup of citric acid, may be used.

VALUABLE TOOTH WASH.

Gum guaiacum.
Orris root, of each one ounce.
Camphor gum, one drachm.
Put these ingredients in a pint of good brandy; let the mixture infuse for ten days, shaking it occasionally; then strain the mixture through a cotton cloth into a clean bottle.

Wash and cleanse the teeth once in twenty-four hours with this preparation, and bleeding, enlarged or detached gums will be healed, lessened and restored in their proper place, and the tooth-ache will seldom be experienced. This is the most valuable preparation we have ever used.

TOOTH-ACHE.

For immediate relief:
Oil of cloves.
Oil of cinnamon.
Creosote, of each half drachm.
Chloroform, half ounce.
Mix.

Take a tuft of cotton wound around the end of a little stick; saturate it in the mixture, and bathe the gum on each side of the tooth with the medicine. If the tooth has a cavity, put a piece of cotton saturated with the medicine in it. This will smart and burn for a little while, but no matter; it will cure the tooth-ache.

MISCELLANEOUS.

Tablespoonful of the juice of a roasted lemon, sweetened to taste, is an excellent remedy for coughs, taken every two or three hours.

The juice of one lemon to half glass of water,

sweetened a little, used as a gargle, will cure many mild cases of diphtheria, a little swallowed each time is all the better.

With the juice of two lemons added to a gill of water and one of brandy, applied externally, we have cured many cases of erysipelas after all other remedies had failed.

The juice of one lemon, sweetened to taste, half a teaspoonful taken every fifteen minutes, has cured many cases of sick headache.

Lemonade is also an admirable drink for all kinds of fevers.

It is also a refreshing drink for those who are well, when tired and thirsty.

Equal parts of lemon juice and glycerine will, ordinarily, remove tan and freckles from the face and hands. Try it.

MAGNETIC LOTION, OR LINIMENT, FOR THE BODY.

Oil of amber,
Oil of lavender,
Oil of origanum,
Oil of sassafras,
Oil of spearmint, of each, half ounce;
Oil of olives, one ounce;

Spirits of turpentine, half ounce;

Aqua ammonia, half ounce;

Tincture of opium, one ounce;

Alcohol, not quite one pint.

Mix.

This lotion is excellent for bathing the chest or the entire body of those who have weak lungs, or any one from loss of vitality; it is splendid for all kinds of sore throat; bathe the throat well, then saturate a flannel with the medicine and pin it around the throat. Some of our patients have pronounced this remedy splendid for rheumatism, or sprains, and weak back.

MAGNETIC LINIMENT, FOR RHEUMA-TISM, SPRAINS, OR STIFF JOINTS.

Oil of lavender,

Oil of sassafras,

Oil of cedar,

Oil of origanum,

Oil of spearmint,

Aqua ammonia, fff, of each, two ounces.

The whites of three eggs, well mixed with half a pint of alcohol. Dilute part of it with water, pour on the eggs, little at a time, and shake hard; then pour on a little more and shake, and so on, as the alcohol will cook the eggs if it is poured full strength and all at once. After the eggs are well amalgamated, add the balance of the ingredients; then add half an ounce of tincture of camphor. Shake well every time you use it, as the mixture sepa- rates on standing. This is the most valuable lini- ment ever given to the world for this purpose. It must be kept well corked, or the medicine will evaporate. Apply it with the hand, and rub in well. Don't be in a hurry; take plenty of time in applying it; the medicine is slow in penetrating the muscles and membranes. The author has made many remarkable cures with this liniment, after all hopes of the patient have fled.

POISON OAK, OR IVY.

Cosmoline, one ounce;
Bromine, one-half drachm.
Mix.

Apply to the affected parts two or three times a day. Wash the medicine off twice a day with a little castile soap and soda water. On going to bed apply the medicine thoroughly. Warm the cosmo- line, so the bromine will mix well; keep the bottle well corked, and setting bottom side up, as the bro- mine escapes upward.

FOR THE ITCH.

Oil of bergamot, half ounce;
Glycerine, one and one-half ounces.
Mix.

Apply in the evening and wash off in the morning with a little soda water and soap. Pleasant and effectual. (Dr. Younkin.)

Homœopathic.—This disease is caused by very small parasites investing the cutaneous surface; and in order to cure it radical external treatment must be given; general friction of the whole body; after being thoroughly washed with hot soap suds for half an hour, dry with a towel; then anoint the body all over with a preparation of lard, 300 gms.; flour sulph., 50 gms.; subcarb. of potash, 25 gms. Apply on going to bed; take another bath in the morning; continue the treatment for three successive nights, and, if necessary, repeat. Your druggist will prepare it for you. In addition to this, we select some remedies to aid the external treatment: Arsen., Sulph., Carbo. veg., Phyto., Sepia., Hep. sulph., Rumex. crisp., Apis. Prepare and take in the usual way.

POISONS AND THEIR ANTI-DOTES.

Nothing that pertains to domestic treatment is of greater value than a knowledge of poisons and the treatment necessary in cases of accidental or premeditated poisoning. So many substances of a poisonous nature are used in manufactures, among farmers and mechanics, and also in private houses, that it will be useful to have a guide to refer to in case of accident, for in almost every case of poisoning the antidote must be instantly given or else relief cannot be expected.

As a general rule, in all cases of poisoning, especially if seen immediately after the poison is swallowed, the first thing to do is to make the person *vomit*. To bring this about, give a teaspoonful of mustard in a tumbler of water, or two or three teaspoonfuls of powdered alum in the same way. *Vomiting* can in all cases be promoted by tickling the throat with a feather.

ARSENIC.

ARTICLES.—Scheele's green, arsenious acid, arpiment, King s yellow, realgar, fly powder, arsenical paste and soap, rat poison.

SYMPTOMS.—Pain and burning in the stomach, dryness of throat, cramps, purging, vomiting, hoarseness and difficulty of speech, eyes red and sparkling, suppression of urine, matter vomited greenish or yellowish.

TREATMENT.—Give large quantities of milk and raw eggs, lime water, or flour and water; then castor oil, or if tincture of iron is within reach, take from half to a full teaspoonful of it, and mix with a little bi-carbonate of soda or saleratus, and administer it to the patient, and follow with an emetic. This acts as a real antidote—the chemical combination being insoluble in the fluids of the stomach.

COPPER.

ARTICLES.—Blue copperas, blue verditer, mineral green, verdigris, food cooked in copper vessels, pickles made green by copper.

SYMPTOMS.—Coppery taste in the mouth, tongue dry and parched, very painful colic, bloody stools. convulsions.

TREATMENT.—Large quantities of milk and white of eggs, afterwards strong tea. *Vinegar should not be given.*

17

IRON.

ARTICLES.—Sulphate of iron (copperas), green vitriol, chloride of iron.

SYMPTOMS.—Colic pains, constant vomiting and purging, violent pain in throat, coldness of skin, feeble pulse.

TREATMENT.—Give an emetic, afterward magnesia or carbonate of soda and water; also mucilaginous drinks.

LEAD.

ARTICLES.—Acetate, or sugar of lead, white lead, red lead, litharge.

SYMPTOMS.—Metallic taste in mouth, pain in stomach and bowels, painful vomiting—often blood, hiccough. If taken for some time, obstinate colic, paralysis—partial or complete, obstinate constipation, diminution of urine.

TREATMENT.—Put two ounces of epsom salts into a pint of water and give a wineglassful every ten minutes until it operates freely.

PHOSPHORUS.

ARTICLE.—Lucifer matches.

SYMPTOMS.—Pain in stomach and bowels, vomiting, diarrhea, tenderness and tension of the abdomen, great excitement of the whole system.

TREATMENT.—Prompt emetic, copious draughts of warm water containing magnesia, chalk, whiting, or even flour. *No oils or fat should be given.*

OPIUM.

ARTICLES.—Laudanum, paregoric, black drop, soothing syrups, cordials, syrup of poppies, morphine, Dover's powder, etc.

SYMPTOMS.—Giddiness, stupor—gradually increasing to a deep sleep, pupil of the eyes very small, lips blue, skin cold, heavy, slow, breathing.

TREATMENT.—Produce vomiting as quickly as possible. Use mustard and warm water or salt and water; tickle the throat with a feather. After vomiting, give plenty of coffee, and place a mustard poultice around the calf of each leg; if the patient be cold and sinking, give stimulants and rouse him to walking or running by your assistance. Beat the soles of the feet, dash cold water on the face; do anything to prevent him from sleeping until the effects have passed off, for if he goes to sleep it is the sleep of death.

STRYCHNINE.

ARTICLES.—Rat poison, nux vomica. St. Ignatius bean.

Symptoms.—Lockjaw, twitching of the muscles, convulsions, the body is bent backward so as to rest on the feet and head only.

Treatment.—Empty the stomach by an emetic, then give linseed tea or barley water. To an adult give thirty drops of laudanum, to relieve the spasms. A teaspoonful of ether may also be given.

OTHER POISONOUS PLANTS OR SEEDS.

Such as false mushrooms, belladonna, henbane, or anything a child may have eaten; or taken through mistake. Vegetable poisons act either as an irritant, acro-narcotic or narcotic. If it is an irritant, the symptoms are an acrid, pungent taste, with more or less bitterness, excessive heat, great dryness of the mouth and throat, with a sense of tightness; violent vomiting, purging, with great pain in the stomach and bowels, breathing quick and difficult, appearance of intoxication, pupil frequently dilated, insensibility, resembling death. The symptoms of narcotic poisons are described under Opium.

Treatment.—If an irritant, and vomiting does occur and continues, render it easier by large draughts of warm water, but if symptoms of insensibility have come on without vomiting, empty the stomach with any emetic that may be at hand.

After the emetic, give a sharp purgative. After as much of the poison is got rid of as possible, very strong coffee, or vinegar diluted with water, may be given with great advantage. Camphor mixture with a little ether may be frequently given, and if insensibility be great, warmth and friction should be employed.

HOW TO PREPARE POULTICES.

Equal parts of ground flax seed, slippery elm bark and oatmeal, for general purposes, is the best we have ever used. It can be mixed with either hot or cold water, as desired. If the surface is very tender, it is better to be warm when applied. It should be well mixed, so there are no lumps in it; not too thin or too thick. This poultice will keep moist longer than either of the above ingredients by itself. This is the way we prescribe our poultices to be made:

BREAD POULTICE.

Take several slices of bread, pour over them sufficient hot water, and let stand for an hour or so, that the bread may be soft; then pour off the water, and with a fork beat the bread into a thick dough; spread on a piece of linen previously cut the size you wish it. Bread poultices are very valuable for their bland effect for all irritating surfaces.

For gangrenous and bad smelling ulcers or sores of any kind, sprinkle some pulverized charcoal over the ulcer before applying the poultice; it can also be mixed with the poultice. Charcoal poultices correct offensive smells from foul sores, and favor a healthy action.

Poultices are chiefly used in the following complaints: Pneumonia, pleurisy, bronchitis, peritonitis, acute rheumatism, lumbago, and to mature and facilitate the discharges of matter in abscesses, boils, etc. When used to mature abscesses or disperse inflammation, poultices should always extend beyond the surface of the inflamed tissues, but after the inflammation is subdued, and the abscess discharging, the poultice should not be much larger than to just cover the opening through which the matter is escaping; if continued too large, they irritate, and may develop other boils or abscesses around the old one. Poultices over the chest or abdomen should be made very thick, as they dry very soon. They must be well secured by suitable jackets or bandages sufficient to hold them in place. They should be changed often; do not disturb the old one till the new one is ready to be replaced.

Poultices can be made from many different kinds of substances that have valuable medicinal properties.

POTATO POULTICE.

Boil the common potato in the usual way, mash and mix with ground elm bark. This is a valuable poultice for acute inflammatory sore eyes, applied very thin and changed often. Also, the raw, scraped potato, in the shape of a poultice, is very valuable for the same purpose.

MUSTARD POULTICE.

If you wish a very quick action from this poultice, mix the mustard with vinegar alone into a thick paste, spread it on the cloth thin with a case-knife, lay it on the affected parts. It will take effect in a very few minutes. You can oil the skin a little, so the mustard will not stick or annoy your patient. This is the way it should be applied to the soles of the feet, if you expect any benefit from it, and changed often. But if you wish it to work slow, you can mix it with equal parts vinegar and water, and add a little wheat flour to the mustard; spread on your cloth a little thicker than the other way; then lay a very thin piece of linen over the mustard before you apply it to the patient.. A mustard poultice should be kept on from ten to twenty minutes at least, till the skin is drawn very red and is irritable afterwards. It is said that if the white of an egg is mixed with the mustard it will never draw into a blister, and thus it can be kept on longer, which is very beneficial.

HOW TO MAKE FOMENTATIONS.

Fomentations are employed for the purpose of lessening pain and inflammation, and for relaxing the parts. They are usually composed of bitter herbs, steeped for a time in hot water or vinegar and water, then placed in muslin cloth or sacks and applied over the affected parts as hot as can be borne. Care should be taken not to moisten or stain the patient's clothes. They are to be removed often and changed for hot ones; if the pain or inflammation is severe, the oftener they are changed the better.

Hop and vinegar fomentations are very valuable for pain in the head, bowels, or any other part of the body.

St. Johnswort or poke root are very valuable, applied hot to the breasts, to disperse or scatter inflammatory condition, caked breasts or tumors and swellings; the wild indigo fomentation is valuable. The smart-weed is also good.

The mullein fomentation surpasses everything we know of for dispelling bruises or swellings in man or beast. A strong decoction made from the mullein leaves, applied hot or cold, to sprains. We have used it for years with astonishing results.

RULES TO ADMINISTER MEDICINE.

Suppose the dose for an adult to be one drachm:

A child under 1 year will require but one-twelfth, or 5 grains.

"	2 years	"	one-eighth, or 8 grains.
"	3 "	"	one sixth, or 10 grains
"	4 "	"	one quarter,or 15 grains.
"	7 "	"	one-third, or 1 scruple.
"	13 "	"	one-half, or ½ drachm
"	20 "	"	two-thirds, or 2 scruples.

A person over 21 years, the full dose of one drachm.

A person of 75, the inverse gradation of the above.

This is an excellent table for regulating the doses of medicines. A mixture, powder, pill or draught may be proportioned to a nicety by attention to the above rules.

TO MEASURE MEDICINE INSTEAD OF WEIGHING.

A drachm of any substance that is near the weight of water, will fill a common teaspoon level full. Four teaspoonfuls make a tablespoonful, or one-half ounce. Two tablespoonfuls, an ounce, and so on. On the same principle, one-third of a teaspoonful will be one scruple, or twenty grains in weight.

DOSES VARIED ACCORDING TO AGE.

The doses of medicines recommended for an adult (or grown person), may be varied to the age of the patient, according to the following rule:

Two-thirds of the dose for a person from fourteen to sixteen.
One-half   "   "   seven to ten.
One-third   "   "   four to six.
One-fourth   "   "   three years old.
One-eighth   "   "   one year old.

LIQUID MEASURE.

A tablespoonful contains half an ounce;
A pint   "   sixteen ounces;
A teacup   "   one gill;
A wineglass   "   two ounces;
A teaspoonful   "   sixty drops;
Four teaspoonfuls are equal to one tablespoonful.

DRY MEASURE.

A tablespoonful contains four drachms, or half an ounce;
A teaspoonful   "   one drachm;
A teaspoonful   "   sixty grains.

DOSES OF MEDICINE.

The following scale has been established for the regulation of the doses of medicine in general:

If the dose for a person of middle age be one drachm, the dose for one from fourteen to twenty-one years of age will be two scruples, or two-thirds as much.

From seven to fourteen, half a drachm, or one-half.

From four to seven, one scruple, or one-third.

The dose for a child of four years will be fifteen grains, or one-quarter.

For a child three years old, ten grains, or half a scruple.

For two years old, eight grains.

For a year old, five grains, or one-twelfth as much as for a person of middle age.

Women, in general, require smaller doses than men, owing to a difference in size and constitution.

Since the Fluid Extracts and Specific Tinctures have been introduced the doses are much smaller than the above table, but they are of the same ratio as the above scale.

LIST OF HOMŒOPATHIC REMEDIES

USED IN THIS BOOK.

Acid bromicum.
Acid carbolic.
Acid hydrocyanic.
Acid muriatic.
Acid nitric.
Acid phosphoric.
Acid sulphuricum.
Aconitum nap.
Æsculus glabra.
Æsculus hippocast.
Ailanthus gland.
Aletrin.
Alnus rubra.
Alunin.
Aloe socatrina.
Alumen.
Aluminium.
Alumina.
Ambrosia.
Ammonium bromide.
Ammonium carbon.

Ammonium muriat.
Ammonium phosph.
Anacardium orient.
Antimon. crudum.
Antimon. iod.
Antimon. arseniate.
Antim. tartaricum.
Apis mellifica.
Apocynum cannabin.
Argentum met.
Argentum nitric.
Arnica montana.
Arsenicum album.
Arsenicum met.
Arum maculatum.
Arum triphyllum.
Asafœtida.
Asclepias inc.
Asclepias tuberosa.
Aurum met.
Baptisia tinct.

Baryta acetic.
Baryta carbon.
Baryta muriatica.
Belladonna.
Benzoic acid.
Bismuthum metall.
Bismuthum nitric.
Borax.
Bromium.
Bryonia alba.
Buchu.
Cactus grand.
Calabar bean.
Calcarea carb.
Calcarea chlor.
Calcarea hypophosp.
Calcarea jod.
Calcarea phosphor.
Camphora.
Camphor mon., B.
Cantharis.
Capsicum annum.
Carbo animalis.
Carbo vegetabilis.
Carbolic acid.
Caulophyll. thalict.
Caulophyllin.
Causticum.
Cedron.

Cepa.
Chamomilla.
Chelidonium majus.
Chelone glabra.
Chimaphila umb.
China off.
Chionanthus virg.
Chloral. hydrat.
Cimicifuga racem.
Cina.
Cinchona off.
Cocculus.
Coccus cacti.
Cochlearia armora.
Coffea cruda.
Colchicum Autumn.
Collinsonia Can.
Colocynthis.
Conium maculatum.
Copavia off.
Corydalis formosa.
Cosmolin.
Crocus sativa.
Cubeba off.
Cuprum acetic.
Cuprum carbonic.
Cuprum met.
Digitalin.
Digitalis purp.

Dioscorea vill.

Dulcamara.

Erigeron Canad.

Ergotin.

Eucalyptus glob.

Euonymus atrop.

Euonymus Europæus.

Eupatorium purp.

Ferri brom.

Ferrum met.

Gelseminum nitid.

Gentiana aquifolium.

Geran maculatum.

Glonoinum.

Graphites.

Grindelia robust.

Guarana.

Hamamelis virginica.

Helianthus annus.

Helleborus niger.

Helonias dioica.

Hepar sulphus. calc.

Hepar sulph. kalic.

Hydrastis Canaden.

Hydrocyanic acid.

Hyoscyamus niger.

Hypericum perforat.

Ignatia amara.

Indigo.

Ipecacuanha.

Iris versicolor.

Jalappa.

Juglans regia.

Kali bichromic.

Kali brom.

Kali carbonic.

Kali chloric.

Kali permangan.

Kali Hypophos.

Kali phosphoric.

Kreosotum.

Lachesis.

Lachnantes tinct.

Ledum palustre.

Leptandra virg.

Lilium tiginum.

Lithium brom.

Lobelia inflata.

Lycopodium clavat.

Lycopus virginicus.

Macrotis racem.

Melilotus.

Mercur. sol. Hahn.

Mercur. subl. cor.

Mercurius vivus.

Monobromide camph.

Moschus.

Muriat. acid.

Mygale avicularia.
Myosotis.
Natrum carbonicum.
Natrum muriaticum.
Natrum sulphuricum.
Niccolum sulph.
Nitric acid.
Nux moschata.
Nux vomica.
Oleander.
Opium.
Per Manganate of Pot.
Petroleum.
Phosphoric acid.
Phosphorus.
Phosphate of Lime.
Phytolacca decand.
Plantago major.
Platina.
Plumbum carbon.
Plumbum met.
Podophyllum.
Polygala Senega.
Pulsatilla nigricans.
Quinine.
Rhododendron.
Rhus Toxicodendron.
Rhus Rad.
Rumex crispus.

Sabadilla.
Sabina.
Salicin.
Salicyl. acidum.
Sanguinaria Canad.
Sanguinarin.
Santoninum.
Scilla maritima.
Scutellaria laterif.
Scutellarin.
Secale cereale.
Secale cornutum.
Senna.
Sepia.
Silicea.
Silicon.
Soda S. carb.
Sodæ hypophosphas.
Spigelia anthelmint.
Spongia tosta.
Squilla maritima.
Stayphysagria.
Stramonium.
Sulphur.
Sulphur. tinctura.
Sulphuric acid.
Symphytum off.
Tartarus emeticus.
Tartaric acid.

Terebinthina.
Trillium pendulum.
Uranum nitr.
Urtica dioica.
Urtica urens.
Ustillago madis.
Urva ursi.
Valeriana officin.
Veratrum album.

Veratrum viride.
Viburnum opulus.
Xanthoxyl. fraxin.
Yerba santa.
Zinci phosphodium
Zinc brom.
Zincum carbonic.
Zincum met.
Zincum valerian.

GENERAL REMARKS.

The reader of our book will see we have not gone into any description whatever of medicinal plants—as is usually done in all other domestic medical works—for the reason you will see more fully explained in an article on Progress of Medicine, given at the close of our book, which we wish you to read carefully. But, instead, we have given you our Prescriptions, just as we would write them should you come to see us; you can go to the drug store, get the fluid extracts and mother tinctures, which are now made from roots and herbs gathered in their proper season. The science of Botany and Chemistry have taught us how to extract the active medicinal principles from these plants; therefore the manufacturing scientists, who are responsible parties, have now men of science and experience constantly employed gathering these medicinal plants from all over the country, the result of which is that, within the last three or four years, the scientific pharmacies have given to the world a universal standard strength from the active medicinal principles of the medicinal plants. This is a great achievement, a triumph which we have never

18 (273)

known before.   This fact gives to the physician, as
well as the people, the advantages of procuring at
any first-class druggist a pure article of the active
principle of any drug we want.   No matter where
obtained, you can rely upon it as a universal standard of strength.   These drugs are in the shape of
fluid extracts, specific tinctures, the sulphates, resinoids and alcoloids.

This is very desirable, from the fact it makes the
dose so small and much more agreeable to the
taste, the dose being only drops and grains and
fractions of grains, from a half drachm to a drachm,
and far more reliable in its effect.   These are facts
which are certainly very desirable to know, when
we consider, a few years ago, we were in the night
of ignorance, we had to gather the plants regardless of their season, boil and stew them to make
teas and decoctions, which were of the crude material, and pour down the throats of patients whole
teacupfuls, and in many cases a pint for a dose.
Then we were ignorant of the fact that the stomach
and human system must be their own chemical
laboratory, out of which this pint dose, after a great
deal of labor on the part of the stomach, could only
extract about half a drop of the active principle of
the drug, the balance being wholly waste material
that the human system must labor to rid itself of.

Hence, our book is a timely messenger, that you
may know you need not, should not, buy any more

roots and herbs at a drug store, thinking to make your own medicine, for you can't do it; besides, many of these crude drugs have been lying in the store for years, all worm-eaten and dusty, and as worthless as a handful of chips gathered from an old wood-pile, while the active principles of the drug made from the green root gathered in its proper season and manufactured into fluid extract, tincture, etc., will keep for years in well-corked bottles. Hence, you can see, if we have a universal standard of strength agreed upon by the scientific pharmacists, we are safe, since the only competition consists in the different manufacturing houses to see which can outdo the other in furnishing the world from this standard of strength a purer article of drugs, more palatable, and therefore more desirable.

This, dear reader, is the reason we have said nothing about the medicinal plants in our book, but given you our Prescriptions, and directed you to your druggist and have them filled. The cost of these prescriptions in many instances will be much higher than they used to be, on account of their purity. However, what you pay now you will more than save in the quality, as much less in quantity is required.

HYGIENE.

Hygiene differs from medicine, but bears a close relationship to it. Hygiene prevents disease, and medicine cures. It bears a close connection to physiology, which teaches the laws of life and health; to chemistry, which reveals the nature of poisons, whether taken in the air we breathe, the food we eat, or the fluids we drink. Hygiene aims to discover the cause of disease and death, and the means of averting or altering these causes to prevent these calamities. To do this it classifies the factors of life under AIR, FOOD, WATER and HEAT.

There can be no animal life without AIR. The smallest insect needs a supply of oxygen. This it must draw from the atmosphere, and when once obtained, it produces its chemical changes in the interior of the insect. Each living cell of which its body is composed contributes to the aggregate of its life, only as it is acted upon by the oxygen received. It is this fact that lies at the foundation of a thousand inquiries in regard to the ventilation of dwellings, shops, churches, etc.; indeed, of all places where there are living beings. By this great fact we are enabled to explain a large per cent. of disease and death, and the more this is studied and heeded, the more will longevity be promoted, the health of cities and communities enhanced. But we are also to remember the air we breathe not only supplies us with oxygen, but it is the great repository of all the exhalants from the earth, decayed animal and vegetable matter. It comes to us sometimes loaded with poisons. Being absorbed into the blood, they work their destructive action on the body, damaging the functions of life, and often destroying the existence altogether.

WATER is another factor of organic life. Without it no chemical change can take place in the living body. Water enters into all the composition of organized beings. A man that weighs 150 pounds, contains 111 pounds of water in his tissues. All the solid materials of the body are carried to their places by the agency of water. All the higher animals drink water for this purpose; and the adult human being takes, upon an average, from seventy to eighty ounces of water daily. Water is a potent chemical agent; its solvent power is equal to that of the mineral acids, and associates itself with a vast number of compounds. It dissolves both organic and inorganic matter; but it may become so impregnated with poisonous substances as to unfit it for the purposes of life.

The human body requires varied compounds of carbon, hydrogen, oxygen and nitrogen in the shape of FOOD. Air and water of themselves, though they fill an important place in the economy of life, cannot supply the system with elements necessary for the play of chemical forces which result in vital phenomena. The blood must be supplied with chloride of lime, the muscles must have potash, the bile must have sulphur, the saliva cyanogen, the nerves phosphorus, the hair, teeth and nails must have silica. If the diet is deficient, disease will invade the system most certainly. Armies have been starved on an excessive diet of salt beef. Children have been sacrificed by confinement to starchy food. The human body may have too much of one thing and not enough of another. What, then, is a healthy diet? We answer, such as contains the constituents of the human body. Science and instinct both answer this question. They reach the same goal; in this connection comes up the question of nervous stimulants, as tea, coffee, tobacco, opium and alcoholic drinks, for which we have no space in this volume. Suffice it to say, they are not necessary except as medicines.

THE HISTORY AND ORIGIN OF MEDICINE.

Medicine is, no doubt, coeval with the history of human suffering, but as a profession, it first began in the early accounts given of the Egyptians. The priests of the early nations were the practitioners of the healing art, but from all accounts they were exceedingly empirical, making use of but few remedies, the most of which were external applications, together with incantations and ceremonies to affect the imagination, though their efficiency in curing disease was, for the most part, due to their knowledge of a few medicinal principles.

Hippocrates was the first to arrange the principles of medicine into an attempted science, while Æsculapius first made it an exclusive study and practice. Æsculapius flourished about twelve hundred and fifty years before Christ; his two sons became celebrated surgeons in the Greek armies during the Trojan war.

Fifty years after the destruction of Troy, a temple was built in honor of Æsculapius, who was then worshiped as one of the gods.

The worship of this god soon spread throughout

all Greece and passed into Asia, Africa and Italy, so that multitudes of temples were erected in honor to his name, and in which he was worshiped.

These temples were erected in the midst of the most delightful scenery, and statutes of colossal proportions were erected to represent the god of medicine.

Pythagoras first introduced the practice of visiting patients at their homes: (500 years B. C.) He rejected all theories in medicine, and contended that experience was the only safe guide to a successful practice.

About three hundred years before Christ, Ptolemy founded a medical school in Alexandria in Egypt, and among the Ptolemies the most celebrated were Erasistratus and Herophilus, who were the first to dissect the dead. These men opposed blood-letting and the use of all violent remedies and trusted to nature in the cure of disease. They paid particular attention to the action of the heart, and were the first to observe the pulse and its variations.

The Pythagoreans became the dominant school, partly through the earnest efforts of Hippocrates (430 years B. C.) who opened up an earnest warfare upon the superstitious ceremonies of the Æsculapian priests, though he, in his practice, still adhered to bleeding and purging.

Three hundred and twenty years before Christ

the Alexandrian library was formed, which had a happy effect upon the departments of medicine, anatomy and physiology. In this library there were 600,000 volumes or rolls which contained all the valuable information of previous ages.

One hundred and thirty years after Christ, Galen was born in Pergamos, and 500 years after his birth, the Alexandrian library was burned by Caliph Omar. Galen had access to this library; he traveled much and wrote largely on subjects connected with medicine. He was an independent thinker and paid but little heed to what was then called authority. So great was his learning and wisdom that he obtained the reputation of "oracle." He thoroughly studied all the schools of medicine and philosophy, and then selected from all, except from the Epicurians, which he totally rejected. Galen determined to gather from the various sources all that was useful in the treatment of disease. He was, perhaps, the first "eclectic" in the practice of medicine.

From the twelfth to the fifteenth century, the practice of medicine was again confined chiefly to the priests, who were men of learning and who became the principal physicians.

About this time an attempt to investigation was made by a class of men who seemed to think that, while physical science was making some gigantic strides, there was no reason why medical science should be so comparatively slow, but a large majority believed that no progress was possible and hence, to shield their ignorance, they attacked every species of investigation in the most vehement manner, which in the least conflicted with their narrow and illiberal views

In 1628, Harvey discovered the circulation of the blood, for which he was called the "circulator" in derision. He was deprived of the right to practice medicine, and was threatened with banishment. He was finally compelled to leave his native country, to escape the obloquy heaped upon him, and he finally died without seeing the benefits of his investigations.

In 1638, the wife of an ex-king of Peru was persuaded, while suffering with a malarial fever, to try the cinchona, and was afterwards restored to health. Ten years after, a Jesuit endeavored to introduce the Peruvian bark in Europe ; he was denounced as a quack, and the common people were persuaded to believe that the bark created disease instead of curing it

PRESENT MEDICAL SCHOOLS.

The different philosophies of ancient times have given rise to different theories, and hence in our times we have different medical schools, each of which base their practice upon the peculiar philosophy they have adopted. It will not be out of place now to give a short description of the peculiar features of medical schools of the present day. Of these, we have the Allopathic, Homœopathic, and Eclectic as the chief, while there are minor schools, as the Botanic, Hydropathic, etc., etc.

THE ALLOPATHIC SCHOOL.

This school of medicine comprises a large class of the physicians of the present day. They are known as "old school doctors," "mineral doctors," "calomel doctors," "allopaths," and "regulars." They are justly entitled to the term "old school," for their present treatment does not materially differ from that of Hippocrates, who flourished twenty-two centuries ago.

They base their practice upon the Latin maxim, *Contraria Contrarius Curanter*, which implies that disease must be cured by antagonism—that if a person have a disease, another disease should be set up in the system, contrary to the one already there, and in this way they attempt to modify diseased conditions. For this, they frequently gave calomel to salivate the system, and by this salivation they expected to counteract the already existing disease. Later years, many of this school have modified their views upon this subject, hence they endeavor to avoid the force of their Latin motto.

Though at first they gloried in the name of Allopatha, many of them now despise the name, on account of the force of its meaning (Allopathic is from the Greek *allos*—other, and *pathos*—disease; other disease), and hence they choose to be known by the somewhat exclusive title of "regulars."

While there is a modification in these respects, there is a disposition to adhere to the old landmarks, hence the philosophy remains the same; but their practice seems to be gradually leaving the old path. The Allopathic profession of to-day is not what it was forty years ago in many respects. A very large class of this school are in favor of progress and improvement, and in keeping up with the times, while others seem to think profession should be stereotyped into a general routine.

This school gives medicine in sensible doses and pays but little attention to the taste. Their medicines for the most part are drastic and powerful, on which account much objection has been raised by the weak and delicate.

BOTANICAL SCHOOL.

It will be needless to say much concerning this system of practice, as it is almost extinct. The physicians of this school are known as " vegetable doctors," " root doctors," " herb doctors," " Indian doctors," " steam doctors," " botanics," " Thompsonians," and, later, "physiopaths." Dr Thompson started out with an utter disgust for the old methods of practice. He inveighed against the use of minerals, and chose the vegetable kingdom as his field for medicinal agents. Some good has been accomplished by Thompson and his followers, but the system never rose from its infancy. Thompson himself was quite illiterate, and the system was crude and could not bear the tests of sound philosophy. Its method of curing disease was by severe drenching, with hot and nauseating teas, made from the common roots and herbs. The system never became very popular, owing to its proscriptive principles and its severe method of treating disease.

HOMŒOPATHIC SCHOOL.

Owing much to the objectionable features in Allopathy, a new system arose upon a philosophy advocated by Hahneman, the Latin term of which is *similia Similibus Curantér*, by which they mean that medicines which produce upon the healthy subject certain diseased conditions, are also capable of curing similar diseases as they arise spontaneously. They claim that "the medicine sets up in the suffering part of the organization an artificial, but somewhat stronger, disease, on account of its great similarity and preponderating influence, takes the place of the former, and the organism from that time forth is affected only by the artificial complaint. This, from the minute doses of medicine, soon subsides and leaves the patient altogether free from disease."

A person in reading this might suppose that the differences between the above schools were but slight; but there is a vast difference and a great gulf between them. The Allopath would think it beneath his dignity to counsel with a Homœopath, this the Homœopath seems to care but little about, while he flatters himself to be the more successful of the two.

The minute doses of medicine in the Homœopathic practice are made by diluting or attenuating their drugs in a systematic way so as to decrease their potency in a geometrical manner. Their medicines do not differ from the Allopathic so much in kind as they do in amount and manner of preparing. They aim to please the palate, which is certainly a commendable feature, when it can be done without sacrificing the disease for the taste. For instance, where the Allopath would give ten grains of calomel, the Homœopath would take but one grain of the drug, and to this he would add sugar of milk and make a hundred grains. He sometimes gives a millionth or a quintillionth part of a grain or drop. Here, then, is the great difference.

Their method of obtaining these minute doses consists in reducing the solid to a powder, and mixing one grain of it with ninety-nine grains of sugar of milk—this is called the first attenuation. The second attenuation is obtained by mixing one grain of the first with ninety-nine grains of sugar of milk; and the third by mixing one grain of the second with the same quantity of sugar of milk, as before. In this way Hahneman proceeded to the thirtieth attenuation. Water is the dilutent of the liquid medicines, and the attenuations are obtained in the same manner—that is, by mixing one drop of the mother tincture or liquid with ninety-nine drops of water, and in this manner continue the dilutions up to thirty, as in the case of solid substances.

These are called first, second and third potencies. Thus they continue, always taking one grain of the last trituration and mixing it with ninety-nine grains of sugar of milk, until they get up to the five-thousandth potency. The liquids or tinctures are treated in a similar manner, though drops are used instead of grains, and alcohol is used instead of sugar of milk.

There is much difference of opinion among the homœopaths in the use of their potencies. Some use the 1st, 2d and 3d potencies, while others practice with their 30th, and others contend for the 200th, while a fourth class declare better results in the use of the 500th.

While some things in homœopathy may appear quite vague and ethereal, as a general thing there is to be found quite a liberal and progressive spirit among them, hence they have a wide range of medicinal agents, and some of the late discoveries in medicine are due to the progressive spirit of homœopathy.

There is no denying the fact that too much strong medicine has been used in former days, and we should hail with delight that spirit which has for its object the improvement of medical science.

ECLECTIC SCHOOL.

We cannot describe this school any better than Dr. Younkin, of St. Louis, has. He says:

"The Eclectics are becoming quite a popular class of medical practitioners. They have at this day a bright galaxy of scholars, philosophers and philanthropists, who are devoting themselves with zeal and industry worthy of all praise to the study and practice of medicine and surgery. Their colleges of learning are becoming somewhat numerous, and their written volumes on the different branches of medical science adorn the libraries of almost all physicians of the different schools. Theirs is a science made up by an inductive system of reasoning. They have added to their storehouse of knowledge, by an earnest study of all the

various systems, and selecting such agents as have
been proven good and useful in whatever school
they could be found. In taking their survey, they
saw much to be condemned and much to be com-
mended in all the schools of medicine, hence they
chose to found a new basis of medical practice in
which should be incorporated the good of all
schools, while the bad should be rejected. They
belong to the progressive class, and claim that none
should be so bound up in theories as not to receive
truth wherever found, whether

‘ In Christian lands, or on heathen grounds.’

"They combine the sweetness of homœopathy
with all that is good in allopathy, hydropathy, or
botanic practice, as well as many discoveries of
their own. Their progress for the last fifteen
years has been surprisingly great, so much so that
even their old standard authors are claimed to be
behind the times. Their present mode of treating
disease is very nearly as pleasant as in homœopathy, and they claim that the power of their agents
will reach the disease more readily, and cure the
patient in a much shorter time than either of the
former schools. The per cent. or death-rate is
claimed not to be as great as in the statistics of
other schools.

On account of the word ECLECTIC, some of the
common people have thought that it had some-
19

thing to do with electricity, but this is not the case. They use electricity as they use any other agent, but they do not use it as their exclusive right. ECLECTIC means SELECT. They aim to select the best of all.

The medicines they employ in the treatment of disease are such agents as will restore the healthy action of all the organs of the human body. They endeavor to avoid the violent and irritating drugs, believing they tend to produce disease and prostrate the system. They seek to support the system and not depress it. They nourish their patients instead of starving them. They aim to restore the healthy action of the liver, kidneys, stomach, and intestines, by assisting nature to throw off disease.

Eclecticism has for its basis the laws of physiology and hygiene. It enjoins upon its practitioners a careful study of all the functions of the body, and teaches that disease is a departure from healthy action, produced either by "excess, defect or perversion."

To relieve a patient from disease, they teach that the first thing is to know the symptoms, and their cause; secondly, to have a thorough knowledge of the effects of remedies, and just what drug is specially indicated in the individual case; the latter of which is obtained by a thorough study of all the materia medica taught by the different schools of medicine.

They use counter irritants, but they seldom blister; they use opiates to relieve pain, but they do not depend upon them as means of cure; they use but few drugs that cannot be readily eliminated from the system.

We have no doubt there has been more *progress* in medical science within the last ten years than within the last hundred. More especially has this been in the direction of furnishing to the world a purer article of medicine—fluid extracts, specific tinctures, resinoids,. alcaloids, etc., the active principle from all medicinal substances— and with it has come to us a better knowledge of how to employ them than was ever known before. Therefore, it will be appropriate for us to note the fact, that in all domestic medical books for the use of families, the crude remedies, roots and herbs, prepared in decoctions, or teas, have been recommended, to which we have serious objections, which we will explain and make plain to our readers.

Through the aid of chemical science, we have learned that the medicinal properties of a plant, which of course means any part of it which is to be used, depends entirely upon the time in the season—we mean the time in the year—when it is gathered, it is known by experience the healing properties are best. Then, again, the healing properties are subjected to the contingencies of the season. We will endeavor to illustrate our meaning. If, for instance, the best time for gathering a plant is in the month of September, then this statement is made in the sense that the season has been of the most favorable condition for producing the healthiest properties of the plant (for plants can be sickly, you know), if the season has been more dry than usual, or more wet than common, it will be perceived at a glance that the remedy gathered one year will be of an entirely different strength than the same remedy gathered in another year, or in a different locality, county and soil. Hence they cannot be made reliable if you should make them into decoctions or teas. Therefore, it has been the aim of our great modern chemists and observers and pioneers to give to the world a system of remedial agents that will be uniform; that is, all manufacturers shall give to the world the solid or fluid extracts, specific tinctures, resinoids, and alcaloids all of equal strength, and at all times, which can be relied upon; if the dose of the remedy be ten drops to produce its medicinal effect, it will be the same all over the world; also, that the same dose shall produce the medicinal effect next year it did this year. Hence, our experience and our confidence has led us to rely upon the tinctures, fluid extracts, alcaloids, etc., etc., which the leading manufacturers in the United States have furnished. Our manufacturers of these botanical remedies have carried off the palm of excellence and superiority everywhere they have been placed in competition with the celebrated manufacturers of Europe at all the great international exhibitions of our day.

These are the reasons why we have advised you all through our book to get your druggist to fill your prescriptions for you. Copy them off, or, better still, take your book to the druggist and show him which prescription you want filled, then you need fear no mistake. In this sense our book is new and its style entirely original. Therefore, we commend this reasoning to the common sense and good judgment of our readers.

In the early days of medical progress in this country, the eminent Dr. Warren, who founded the first Allopathic college in the City of Boston, in one of his medical books, in the most beautiful language has paid the highest tribute to the Eclectic school of medicine that we ever heard. We feel our book would not be complete without giving you some extracts taken from his book, which was published in 1858. He says :

"There is a large and growing class of physicians, called at first, after the founder of the school, Thompsonian. Subsequently they were known as the Botanic physicians, and now pass under the title of Eclectics. These men, directing their attention at first chiefly to the Cayenne and the Lobelia, have greatly extended their zealous researches over the vegetable kingdom, and have gathered much information worthy to be preserved. These researches have revealed a sadly neglected duty on the part of the old school practitioners, and in 1852 drew from the Committee on Indigenous Medicinal Botany, appointed by the American Medical Association, the confession that our practitioners generally have been extremely ignorant of the medicinal plants even in their own neighborhoods, and to this fact the committee attribute it that the Eclectic physicians had in many cases supplanted the Regulars in the confidence of the people. The education and talent of this class of practitioners have gradually risen year by year, till at the present time they have several medical schools, where students are well instructed by men of real ability. The vast list of valuable remedies that these men have given to the world, drawn wholly from our own home plants, are a boon of no small value. I regard them as equal in value to all we were previously in possession of. And yet it is very mortifying that the remedies which these men have given us are by hundreds of our old school practitioners not even known by name, and even where they are known, generally not honored with a trial. 'King's American Dispensatory,' a book of 1,300 pages, in which these plants are well described, is almost unknown among us. Aside from a copy in my own library, I do not know that one is owned by any other member of the Massachusetts Medical Society. However learned a man may be, he is not fully equipped as a practitioner without his full acquaintance with this class of medicines.

[We will add that this valuable book, King's Dispensatory, is not owned nor known much about by one in a hundred old school practitioners, even at this late date, 1881.]

"On the whole, I am disposed to regard all the operators and provers in the different departments of medicine as useful in a degree, no matter to what school they belong, or what class of men, except those mercenary quacks who lie about their remedies to make money. But all who are sincere and honest and believe what they teach, are aiding in some measure the general advancement of science. Although the truths, as they present them, are but fragmentary, they may prove useful in the hands of the true, liberal and progressive men who have chosen for themselves the name and title of Eclectics, which means all those men who have the wisdom as well as the independence to select the best things out of all systems of medicine. And that brings us to remark that the general conclusion must be there is but one truly liberal and philosophical school of medicine, and that is the Eclectic, composed of that class of thinking men who have liberality enough, as well as independence, to reject all and every exclusive system of medicine, and receive out of all systems only those things which are approved by experience and reason.

PROGRESS OF MEDICINE.

There have been long periods when the science and art of healing made scarcely any progress; but now they are advancing, and in some departments rapid. The chemistry in man—commonly called animal chemistry—has opened up many sources of light, which in the past were unknown. And but very few physicians have yet commenced the study of these very essential branches of medical science; but the delinquents are but sleeping in the rear of this rapid advance, and will soon awaken to find themselves but the ghosts of a dead generation.

Liebig, a distinguished student in chemistry, has made many very valuable discoveries to open the way for inquiry into this department. Simons, also, has perhaps done more. Mealhe is exploring still deeper, and has made many valuable discoveries, of which the students of medicine will have these problems before their minds, bye and bye, and they will be compelled to act on them and govern their actions upon them as well—inquiries and propositions like the following :

What are the chemical compositions of the solids and fluids of the human body?

What is the nature of the changes which occur in the composition of the solids and fluids during disease?

What alterations in the chemical compositions of the solids and fluids take place during the operations of medicine before it can exert any remote action on the animal economy?

A remedy must be absorbed, and before it can be absorbed, it must be soluble in the fluids of the human body.

Medicines are subject to chemical changes during their passage through the system.

These changes are regulated by ordinary chemical law, and may, therefore, to some extent, be protected and made available in the cure of disease. Then, again, those laws are disturbed and varied to some extent by the law of vitality; just as the needle is disturbed and made to vary by disturbing forces.

What are those disturbances, and to what extent and under what circumstances do they occur? With these and similar inquiries and propositions before the intelligent physician's mind, diligently studied, the physician will learn, in time, to prescribe with some intelligent aim.

He will not know everything, to be sure, but what he does know he will have a rational reason for knowing.

If he gives a medicine with these facts before him, he will have in view the chemical changes of the solids and fluids of the body known to be dis-turbed by disease, which he is trying to combat.

He will, at the same time, try and keep in mind the solution of medicine in the fluids of the body, as well as the chemical reactions between the com-ponent parts and the acids and alkalies, etc., found in the alimentary tubes and elsewhere.

As the science of medicine advances and be-comes progressive in its march and eclectic in its character, gathering from all systems the best attested facts, and learning to use them to the ex-clusion of all systems of mere theories, and liberal sufficient to hold the present facts in subordination to future experience, then, and not till then, will the medical profession be progressive. With such men as these, the science of medicine will ad-vance, and the light of to-morrow will then be modified by the light of to-day. Such men as these will everywhere be found knocking at the door for admission into some new department of Nature.

NEED OF LIBERALITY.

The medical profession, to be real physicians, must be free from bigotry; they must have no narrow prejudice against any man or class of men, be always ready to examine carefully and candidly any new remedy that is brought to their notice, no matter from what source it may come. They must not hedge themselves about with such restrictive by-laws and society rules as are calculated to fetter their thoughts; that will turn their investigations by a sort of moral necessity into the narrow channels of mere party conservatism.

Remember, he that is once inclosed by such restrictions must hew a path for his feet through bigotry and malevolence itself, before he can escape them, or be a free man in any noble sense. When the professors of the healing art can hoard medical knowledge as misers hoard gold, and can submit its purity to equally certain tests, then it will be time and appear in better taste for them to grow exclusive. Until then the most becoming badge they can wear would be that of the Christian adage, " Let each esteem others better than himself." Medical science with liberal by-laws, fitted to do a great deal of good, but it will be hard to show those with stringently restrictive rules operate otherwise than as a check upon progress. In truth, they are apt to become mere catacombs in which to embalm dead ideas of the past. They are liable to become the instruments for accomplishing the ambition of a few leading, narrow, conservative men with brainless heads, who attempt to suppress everything of a progressive

nature which should happen to be outside of their
organization, and they beget a feeling that would
forbid the fixed stars from shedding a drop of
their light into our atmosphere, without first coming down and joining the solar system.

CONSERVATIVE LEADERS.

There is no influence which holds so steady a
check upon medical progress as conservative lead-
ers in many of our medical associations; not that
they are opposed to any improvement in medical
art, nor would they object to any amount of discovery if it would only come to the profession
through channels which they have the honor of
opening, but against all light from outside or from
obscure sources they will draw down the curtain
and close the doors; and if it should chance to get
within their sacred inclosure, they will call it dark-
ness, and the priests of the temple to atone for the
indignity offered to the gods of medicine, and fill
the whole sky with murky clouds from their altars.
These men have strong faith in cast; therefore, in
low places of society they look for nothing but
ignorance and poverty, notwithstanding the light
of every natural day breaks in the horizon and
ascends.   They so far despise analogies as to insist
that all medical light breaks at what they call the

zenith of the profession, and comes down. With them the temples of Esculapius are all rebuilt and they are the priests, and, therefore, to offer in sacrifice the smallest part of a medical plant is sacrilege, unless it is intrusted to their hands. These are the men who regard knowledge as a contraband article, unless regularly entered at the custom house, with bills of lading properly certified to by the conservative magnates at some other metropolis. With them knowledge is not like the west wind, fanning the brow of the peasant as gently as that of a king; not like the bright light of heaven, entering the small, clean window of the the hut as readily as the large one of the palace; not as a boon, which comes alike freely to all; and which is to be everywhere amplified, changed as circumstances and conditions require, and adapted to the present hour. We would not be unjust or severe, but we cannot but remark further, that these men present but one view to humanity— they are monotonous objects of inspection. Look at them a thousand times and you see but the same unaltered phase of life.

And to the mariner on life's ocean, they are not safe lights to go by, for if he approaches them on the dark side they remain just as black as night, unless he should come around to their shining front. They are not revolving lights; they have lights, to be sure, and may be bright and genial, but it only gleams out upon the waters in one direction; it does not sweep around and throw its direct rays upon every mariner's path. Such men as these can only be useful to a few and a certain class. They have in them no true omniology; they are not all-teaching; their lives are not all-instructive, only to their friends, their clique, party, or school. They have length, but not breadth. They are citizens of Boston, New York, Philadelphia or Cincinnati; but not of the world.

THE TRUE PHYSICIAN.

How different the character of a true man or a physician. He has no dislikes or antipathies, and hates no man except bigots and tyrants. He accepts knowledge although it comes from the humblest of sources; believes that there is no experience but that will repay a careful study of it. He believes there is no husbandman's plowshare but will turn soil that is worth the analyzing. He belongs exclusively to no' party, and can be easily approached by respectable men of every stamp, whether belonging to the same party, school, or society. You can easily take hold of his nature and draw it out without having it slip from your fingers and fly back from your presence into a thousand kinks, just like an over-twisted string.

He is a whole man. God made him for the whole world and not for a party. But, by some strong influence you may draw him from the world for a time into some narrow sphere, but not only will his reluctant nature, like a returning tide, run back continuedly to embrace the continent, and, like a full sea, come back boiling and bubbling and running over.

WHAT WE WANT.

In order that medical knowledge may increase its liberality in the true and full sense, we want true men in high places, who will not only let their own light shine everywhere, but will cease to hinder other light from shining. Beyond this, and of equal importance, we want the medical Gems of Knowledge diffused among the people; we want what the world has never seen before—a popular medical literature. We want the Temple of Esculapius pulled down and these conservative priests turned into the street and become teachers of the multitude, rather than the worshipers of the inner sanctuary. We do not think it necessary to confine knowledge, save in the ministers of religion. Why should not the layman who follows his plow or shoves the plane, become eminent theologians? And why should they not study the lower branches of science which relate to the body? They have never done it heretofore, because it has been purposely hidden from them under technicalities, when these covers should have been torn from them. And will be in the very near future, for when men and women are educated properly, as they should be and must be, how the physical temple will be built, and taught how they should take care of it as well, then the soul will need very little doctoring to save it. It is said those who begin to read upon medicine are very apt to imagine themselves afflicted with the various symptoms they find described. Well, to some extent, they may. But it is also true that the light they obtain by reading often relieves their minds of the apprehension which their previous ignorance allowed to prey upon them, just as boys lose their fears of ghosts when the light of the coming morn changes their thoughts to some familiar object. But these conservative physicians oppose the spread of medical knowledge; they fear their services will be less required—I fear upon the grounds of self interest. They think their services will be less sought for.

Now, we do not think of dispensing with the clergy because the people study theology; neither do we cease to employ teachers and practitioners of medicine when each man and woman will study the healing art. The principal change we shall witness in the future will be much larger attainments in knowledge among practitioners, just as ministers now know, and are obliged to know, ten times as much as they did in the dark ages of the past, when the people had no education and were obliged to receive their spiritual teaching from the mouths of these old fossils. The teachers of art or science are obliged to keep in advance of their pupils. Let the study of medicine become popular among the people, then we will have very few ignorant physicians. Quacks will then become one of the impossibilities. The eclectic and the homœopathic as well as all true physicians believe in scattering medical books among the people, stripped of their technicalities.

Diffuse Gems of Knowledge, and you will find the people will purchase very few of the secret advertised medicines, nor employ quacks as their family physicians.

20

PHILOSOPHY OF HUMAN MAGNETISM.

This is a very common superstition among popular medical men of all schools, that the intellectual
phenomena of Magnetism (or Mesmerism) are the
concomitants of hysterical states of the nervous
system. Old-line doctors attempt to transcend the
otherwise insurmountable difficulties of Somnambulism, or Clairvoyance, by the assumption of im-
posture, or else by charging the mental manifestation to nervous or cataleptic condition of body and
brain. But it is generally believed the majority
of those old-line physicians are pretty well supplied with ignorance concerning many of the most
vital processes of the physical organization.
Chemistry has recently enriched the physicians'
understanding of physiological phenomena, but
does not unravel to his mind the wondrous dynamic
of the feelings and thinking principles which animate and govern the perfect and beautiful organism
of man and woman. The mental and spiritual
phenomena of magnetism are yet new to most
physicians, therefore we do not expect anything
else from them than expressions of professional

prejudices emphasized by strong marks of dogmatic denunciations. But here and there we find a broad-hearted and knowledge-loving physician who is capable of putting a rational question with an honest incredulity, who is ever ready to exchange his learned errors for new truths—willing to make progress in scientific facts, and thus unfurl the union banner of free thought and unlimited invest-igation. But in this little explanation it can hardly be expected of us to construct an argument for the establishment of electro-magnetic science; we can scarcely believe that such an argument is demand-ed by the so-called scientists of the age, and yet we know that no class is more in the rear of ad-vanced discovery than the graduates of our insti-tutions of learning. Many of our best students in medicines are unable to solve the first principle of magnetic phenomena. They treat the facts as obviously incredible and impossible, and so permit themselves to be sufficiently logical to reject the facts, and sometimes uncivil enough to insult the hewers of wood and drawers of water, who have the audacity to present such phenomena for scien-tific examination. In fact, the churches and col-leges are both behind the essentials of knowledge and civilization. The unscientific people, the non-professional observers of nature, and the clear-eyed matronly nurse of the sick-room, are the uncon-scious champions of scientific progress.

After these, like a loaded omnibus behind the laboring horses, come the respectable hosts of physicians and clergymen riding and enjoying themselves luxuriantly in the cushioned chairs of our colleges and evangelical institutions. Millions upon millions of human beings, as well as creatures of the lower grade of animals, breathe the breath of life all unconscious of science, unmindful of the chemical knowledge which would explain the composition of the atmosphere, and reveal the proportions of oxygen and nitrogen to the thoughtless multitude. So it is in every other respect. The people intuitively illustrate the essential facts of science for centuries in advance of the accurate knowledge of the schools. In *human magnetism* this remark is emphatically true. The people with little or no education are familiar with its essential facts, and have practiced the principles of this science long eras before the colleges reflected a single ray of light upon the subject. In fact, the people without education are masters of realities and principles not yet dreamed of in brains of our teachers and professors. For, in truth, what is science? Nothing more or less than systematic observation and orderly arrangement of natural facts and superficial causes which have for hundreds of centuries been common and familiar to some of the inhabitants of every country. It is, therefore, no disadvantage to any experience or philosophy to say that it is not yet accepted and inculcated by talented men in higher places, because we know the knowledge of the colleges and theology of the churches are but reflections of facts and discoveries of past ages.

THE SOURCE OF MAGNETISM,

Or, in other words, *What* is Magnetism ? We answer, it is animal vitality. We use the term Magnetism in its broadest sense, signifying the principle by which one object is enabled to attract, repel and influence another. The *source* of this grand principle is *Soul.* Crystals, various mineral bodies, plants, trees, fish, birds, animals, human beings, each and all are endowed with a soul, which is the mystic life of all boundless nature upwelling and overflowing from the inexhaustible fountain of the First Cause. All students who are intellectually acquainted with the harmonial philosophy will not confound "Soul and Spirit." The term "Soul" is used here to signify that harmonious combination of the principle of motion, life and sensation, which moves, warms and perfects the physical organizations. Stones, trees, animals and men all contain this principle, but the latter in a higher degree of development, while in the former the principle is comparatively dormant. Each natural body of matter is differently capacitated; hence supplied with a soul principle. The consequence of this difference is a magnetic polarity between one body and another throughout the entire domain of nature, and the consequence of this universal polarity is evolution and manifestation of all physical motions and mental phenomena known or unknown to science.

FACTS ILLUSTRATIVE OF MAGNETIC POLARITY

The common magnet, as every one knows, is at once positive and negative; that is, the life of the metallic body makes two manifestations at the same moment, and will attract a negative substance and repel that which is positive to it. The positive pole is charged with negative power, and the negative pole with positive power. Thus the magnetic principle corresponds to these facts. For instance, the seed of a plant is negative to the magnetic ray or heat of the sun; consequently, the properties of the seed, if planted in good ground, leap up toward the sun as naturally as the needle points to the pole. This explains the growth of vegetation. Thus the near relationship of magnetism and electricity is demonstrated; they mutually attract and mutually repel each other. Look at the common electro-magnetic battery. If the electric current is permitted to traverse the coil of wire, it will convert the rod of iron placed in the center into a powerful magnet, and thus in its turn will set in motion a powerful current of electricity, as it were, by way of compensation.

Now, the human body is constituted on the same system of polarities. Man is polarized from side to side, from end to end, from center to surface; his nervous system is a net-work of polarities, from his inmost organic centers to the glands of his brain, and from his brain centers to the extremities of every nerve; he is a perfect battery of magnetic and electric potence. Hence, you can see how easy it is to understand how individuals can affect each other magnetically, and assist in establishing a healthy equilibrium in the magnetical polarities of the human system; for the entire left side from the brain to the toes is negative; the left side emanations are, therefore, tranquil and attractive, while in the right side, which is positive, are powerfully repellant. Hence, man repels, works and destroys with his right side, right arm, hand, leg, foot and brain, while the corresponding parts and members of the left side and brain attract and subdue, and magnetize whatever he is adapted to affect.

The right side of the brain is frequently unimpressible, while the left side may be easily overcome and paralyzed by the magnetic principle of another mind. The right eye in a healthy person is the keenest and best, while the left eye is capable of more pleasureable visions. Also, more susceptible for this reason: it more readily discerns the colors of a substance. The location, size, weight, and the distance of a body are sooner determined by the right eye. If any doubt this, go and experiment with your eyes and senses. Close your left eye and look at the leaf of a plant, then reverse the method, and you will soon see the ray of light emenating from the leaf which your right eye cannot discover.

In like manner your left hand will detect heat in a substance that is cold to the right hand, and the reverse is equally true when frequently practiced with care and discrimination. For these reasons the right hand of man and woman are attractive to each other, while, at the same time, the hand of the same sex are mutually repellant and unwholesome. Clairvoyants can detect the emanations of the different centers by the colors, which is natural to all polarized principles. Clairvoyants can see the magnetic emanations from human bodies when they are in this illuminated state, and such sensitive persons are often repelled away from gross positive minds, and shun them as we would a viper, and our professors of science call such delicate natures weak-minded persons, when the fact is just the reverse. Such minds always have far more intellectual power than the former.

The wonderful complex nervous system of man is a complete helix; a coil of wire which communicates electricity to the brain, which is the magnet, or central power of the organization, and the compensating process as with the electro-battery, goes on in the shape of centrifugal currents of real nerve life (a finer electricity), which the brain discharges through the pneumogastric sympathetic nerves to all parts of the temple. So, in accord with the magnetic law, we come now to observe that the brain and body of the operator becomes one overmastering, positive power, to which, without resistance, the diseased patient surrenders to the positive healthy magnetism of the operator. Thus the complete blending of the magnetic spheres of the twain, the disease in the patient naturally surrenders itself to the healthy body of the operator. Thus, you see, it is only a question of time, either long or short, which must, of necessity, equalize the magnetic soul principle, and both become healthy alike. This magnetic law lies at the foundation of all the so-called Spiritual Phenomena, wherein, to the observer, it seems the spirit or mind of the medium has vacated its temple in order to give a foreign intelligence an opportunity of manifesting itself.

MAGNETISM AS A MEDICINE.

Having briefly sketched the action and effects of
the magnetic principle, it will now be more expe-
dient to conclude our remarks in behalf of the sick
and suffering.   The human body, in its normal
and healthy condition, is endowed with every requisite power.   But by ignorant and negligent
treatment the natural vital forces lose their just
equilibrium, and the effects and consequences are
soon visible in material prostration, in severe pain,
or in silent and insensible decomposition.   What
physicians term " nervous influence " is really
nothing but the magnetic and electric life of the
interior soul.   Animals, including man, have these
magnetic endowments; and the principle of vital
action, in both the human and animal kingdom,
are exactly and universally identical.   A loss of
vital action is nothing but a loss of balance between
inherent forces, which are positive and negative,
magnetic or electric; and yet we do not hold that
the currents generated by the *metallic*, or mineral
battery, can ever be made to act as a substitute, because the principles of *Soul-Life* are as much finer
than atmospheric electricity as the latter is finer
and more delicate than the gross and turbulant
waters of our lakes.

The *Therapeutic* influence of magnetism may
be exerted in various ways, differing in every case,

with temperaments and the nature of the disease; but we cannot stop now to specify any method. We will say, however, that to practice Magnetic Healing successfully, you must have the *will* to do *good*; a firm faith in your power, and an active confidence in employing it. Magnetism is a useful, spiritualizing, sublime agent of vital energy and health. In fact, it is the all-pervading sympathy which connects us with the absolute condition and suffering of our fellow-men. However, we prescribe different remedies merely as palliatives and aids as final redemption from disease, and from the fear of death, but the radical remedy is still within your own individual organization. We have now given you the general principles of the magnetic medicine treasured up in the organs and brain-centers of your own individuality. An inflammation is a positive condition of an organ or part; therefore, apply your positive hand and *will* to it. Why? Because two positives repel, and your hand being a healthy positive, will surely scatter the inflammation, which is an unhealty positive, and thus establish the natural equilibrium. Your brain, for instance, is loaded with blood; not so, your mental magnet is surcharged and overstocked with vital currents which should be engaged in other parts of your economy—and thus the dependent blood is floated off. So our doctors will bleed an apoplextic patient. This method is

absurd. No man's system ever generates more
blood than it needs for its own private use. But it
is possible, nay, easy for the magnetic potencies to
be thrown out of balance, giving rise to co-ordinate
symptoms of excess in one place, and deficiency in
another; the remedy, in all cases, being the same,
viz.: A restoration of the magnetic equilibrium between foot and brain, stomach and liver, heart and
lungs, between spleen and kidneys, and the inevitable consequences will be perfect health.

DR. H. S. TANNER'S FORTY DAYS' FAST.

We feel that our book would not be complete at this late day of discovery and scientific achievements, without giving you a true history of the wonderful fast of forty days, thirteen of which were passed without drink. We glean the following facts from some of the leading medical journals of the day: The Doctor having been criticized for honest assertion of a former fast of forty-two days, by Dr. Hammond, of New York, and others of like belief and persuasion, he took up a temporary residence in New York City, under the charge of the United States Medical College for the purpose of convincing the most skeptical the entire possibility of a man existing forty days without food.

Notwithstanding the Doctor had to brave all former theorizers and the bulwark of "old hunker medicine," he assiduously pursued his attempt, under the most trying ordeal and adverse circumstances, to a successful termination, and on Saturday, August 7, 1880, he completed his fast, the greatest that has ever been authoratively recorded —notwithstanding Dr. Hammond and Dr. Clendenin, Health Officer, Dr. Miles, and many others of the most brilliant shinning stars of the Allopathic school said it could not be done, and pronounced Dr. Tanner a humbug and a fraud.

But long before the Doctor had completed his forty days' fast in New York, the public, generally, was satisfied that he was honestly attempting to carry out what he had undertaken. And those of the profession who at first claimed a fast of forty days impossible, gradually began to change front, and affirm that such facts were not new, that many well-authenticated cases were on record, and they had proved of no benefit to science. After which came the prediction of the knowing ones, that Dr. Tanner would suffer greatly and probably die as soon as he began to take nourishment, for such had been the result of all cases of starvation, and the Doctor could not be an exception to the general rule.

Dr. Tanner always held that fasts of this kind were possible, and one of his objects in undertaking so trying an ordeal was to prove that it could be done. Many cases of fasting have been reported, but they were rarely believed, for the reason no positive evidence of such could be furnished, except that given by the faster. Dr. Tanner, however, accomplished his task under the most rigid system of scrutiny, with the eyes of the whole world upon him. Thus giving positive proof of the possibility of a protracted fast. Therefore, when we have demonstrated that medical authorities are in error regarding the length of time life may be prolonged without food, we are brought face to face with some of the errors we are guilty of in our daily visits to patients, it matters little what the disease may be; we have been disposed to urge the taking of food to sustain life, even if our patient protested against it. This has especially been the custom of the profession, during the last decade, since the supporting and nourishing system of practice came into use. But now it has become a question whether food thus taken when the system did not demand it, had any effect in sustaining life, whether nature is not the best guide after all as to the necessity for food being taken into the stomach.

And now, that it has been demonstrated a person can go ten, twenty, or even forty days without food, then it is our duty to cure the disease by cutting short the irritation, by forcing food upon the stomach when it does not require it. If we have an inflamed eye, we give it rest, and it is rapidly restored. Therefore, the same treatment adopted for disease of the digestive organs must necessarily be followed by equally good results; Dr. Tanner has taught the world that we can abstain from food for a comparatively long period of time without bad results.

Again, leading authorities have taught us that after long abstinence from food the digestive organs are so impared that food must be given in very minute quantities. This practice is adopted in all cases of starvation, and it is a fact that nearly all such patients die. Dr. Tanner has shown that long abstinence does not impair digestion, but that large quantities of nourishment can be taken with impunity. Therefore, a change in this direction promises good results, and should be considered one of the lessons of the fast.

It also demonstrates that even rectal feeding does not sustain life, as has been claimed; but rather that other forces of the body not only keep the patient alive, but also counteract the bad effects of this false method of supposed feeding.

The most important fact proven by this is the wonderful power of mind over matter, as we have tried to explain to you (see article on Magnetism). This fact has demonstrated to science clearly that the human mind is dependent upon some force outside the physical brain. Thus, to our mind, it has only added another link to the chain of evidence we already have, that the mind or spirit, or whatever you wish to call it, does control the body and does live after the body is worn out, and laid away to mingle with the rubbish of the graveyard.

In fact, there are so many points which present themselves for our consideration in this great lesson of the Doctor's fast and feast, that we can do little at present but turn the facts to practical use, and mark out a course for future study, since, after the fast came the feast, when it seems that Dr. Tanner knew the powers of his stomach better than the medical savants, and at once began to partake of large quantities of food from a generous bill of fare, and in four days he gained twenty-four pounds in weight; and on the 31st day of August, just twenty-six days after he completed his fast, he had regained his usual weight and strength, and was as well and hearty as ever.

21

INDEX.